GHANA UNDER NKRUMAH

PHOTO 1959

The First President of Ghana
His Excellency the Right Honourable Kwame Nkrumah, P.C., M.A., M.Sc., LL.D.
September 18, 1909 — April 27, 1972

GHANA
UNDER
NKRUMAH

By

SISTER CHRISTINE X JOHNSON

© Christine X Johnson
All rights reserved. Published 1994
Printed in the United States of America

Other books by Christine Johnson

Muhammad's Children: First Grade Reader. Chicago: University of Islam Press, June 1963.

Poems of Blackness. Chicago: DuSable Museum of African American History, 1970.

Africa's Gift to the World. Chicago: Free Black Press, 1970.

ABC's of African History. New York: Vantage Press, 1970, 1972; reprinted Chicago: 1982, 1988.

Glouba African Masks. Chicago: Reed and Associates, 1983.

ISBN 0-940103-04-4 pb

Christine Johnson
4349 South King Drive
Chicago, IL 60653 USA
312/924-6553

EARL JOHNSON

This book is dedicated to my dear late husband. His courage, struggles and success in providing for, and keeping his family alive and well, was the saga of this Black man in the American colony.

C. X J.

TABLE OF CONTENTS

v	Dedication
ix	Preface *Ohene Boatye*
x	Forward *Dr. Margaret T. Burroughs*
xi	Map of Africa with Ghana inset
xii	State Regalia of Ghana
xv	Stamps of Ghana
xvi	Libation Prayer
xvii	Founders of Ghana
1	Introduction
6	The Saga of Nkrumah

Ghana Under Nkrumah GOVERNMENT

10	African Village Compound
11	Candidates for the Presidency
12	Christianborg Castle
13	Supreme Court Building
14	Accra - General Assembly
15	Accra - House of Parliament
16	The National Assembly
17	The Speaker
18	The Ambassador Hotel

Ghana Under Nkrumah TELEVISION

19	Television for Education
20	The Idea
21	Reading the News
22	Technicians
23	A Discussion in an Accra Studio
24	Training School
25	An Audio Technician
26	Statue of Nkrumah, Founder of Ghana
27	Nkrumah Avenue

Ghana Under Nkrumah AGRICULTURE

28	Cocoa Research Institute
29	Cocoa Nursery
30	Cocoa - The Crop
31	Gathering Cocoa
32	Commercial Cocoa Harvesting
33	Climbing for Palm Nuts
34	Tapping Palm Tree for Wine
35	Palm Nuts
36	The Oil Palm (Elaeis Guineensis)
37	Palm Oil Fruit
38	Oil Palm Fruit Types

Ghana Under Nkrumah COMMUNITY DEVELOPMENT

39	Ghana Young Pioneers
40	Community Center in Accra
41	Community Development
42	Social Welfare
43	Women in Community Development
44	Improvement and Self Help
45	Health Centers
46	Housing Projects
47	Laying Sewers
48	Digging With Hands

Ghana Under Nkrumah TEMA, GHANA

49	Old and New Tema Harbor
51	Fishing in Tema
52	Community Center in Tema
53	Using Primitive Methods
54	Construction in Ghana, Tema Harbor
55	Housing in Tema, a Fishing Village
56	Tema Sailing Club

Ghana Under Nkrumah EDUCATION

57	Educational Policy
58	The Chief's School
59	Primary Schooling
60	Secondary Schools
61	Secondary Boys School
62	Secondary Girls School
63	Secondary High School, Achomoto, Ghana
64	Free Education in Secondary Schools
65	Commonwealth Hall, University College
66	University of Ghana - Legon

Ghana Under Nkrumah PUBLIC WORKS

67	Volta River Dam
68	The Adomi Bridge
69	Akosombo Dam
70	Police Patrol

Ghana Under Nkrumah FACTORY PRODUCTION

71	United Mattress Factory
72	The I.D.C. Match Factory

Ghana Under Nkrumah The MARKET

73	Shallots from Keta Market
74	Bolga Baskets at Keta Market
75	Crops Sold At Market
76	The Makola Market - Accra, Ghana
77	The Salaga Market, Accra Ghana

Ghana Under Nkrumah KENTE CLOTH
 78   Weaving Kente Cloth
 79   Making Kente Cloth

Ghana Under Nkrumah CULTURE
 80   African Drummer
 81   Dancing in Ghana
 82   The Marimba
 83   Dancing to Xylophone Music

Ghana Under Nkrumah TRANSPORTATION
 84   Ghana Airways
 85   Ghana's Own Shipping Line

Ghana Under Nkrumah HEALTH CARE
 86   An African American Visits a Nursing School
 87   Marie Louise Children's Hospital
 88   Kumasi General Hospital

 89   Kumasi Fort
 90   Amy A. Garvey at Home in Kumasi

Ghana Under Nkrumah TRADITION
 91   Asantehene and the Golden Stool
 92   The Soul of Ashanti
 93   Tamale, Ghana
 95   Ghana Chiefs

Ghana Under Nkrumah POLITICS
 96   Hosting Conferences
 97   Women of Africa and African Descent
 98   William E.B. DuBois
 99   World Without the Bomb

 100 Osaygefo, President of Ghana

 101 White Ant Hill

 102 Nkrumah in Chicago, Illinois USA — Photos

 106 Kwame Nkrumah — A Chronology

 110 A Letter Shared

PREFACE

The African Independence Drive was headed by men of vision. There is no human respect without freedom. As said by one of the greatest freedom fighters, Sékou Touré of Guinea "we prefer poverty in freedom to riches in slavery."

Ghana was one of the African Nations who fought for her freedom from Great Britain, under the leadership of Dr. Kwame Nkrumah. He achieved independence for Ghana, the former Gold Coast, from the British colonialism in 1957.

Nkrumah who was educated in the United States made his goals by participating in the liberation of Africa from colonial rule looking toward the unification of all the African Nations, in a United States of Africa. He was elected to Parliament in 1951, then became the Prime Minister in 1952. When Ghana became a Republic in 1960, Nkrumah became its first President, assuming the title, Osagyefo (Redeemer).

Finally, while he was going to Peking on a Vietnam Peace Mission, his Government was overthrown by the army and the police force. He took refuge in Guinea, and in 1972 he died in exile of cancer at the age of 63.

Continually Ghana has been developed unsuccessfully until its present new head of state, Jerry John Rawlings, the President of Ghana.

Today Ghana is in the highlight of development with investors from all over the world. We all thank Dr. Kwame Nkrumah for leading the way into the 21st century.

Ohene Boatye
Student and Native of Ghana

FORWARD

This book, *Ghana Under Nkrumah* by Sister Christine X Johnson is a most welcome addition to the body of literature on Ghana and the life of its first President since Independence, the Honorable Doctor Kwame Nkrumah. Sister Johnson is well equipped to tell this story since she was a personal friend of Nkrumah. She knew him during his student days in the United States. Also she visited and observed the changes in Ghana in the early days of Independence (1957), and the re-building of the country from the ravages of Colonialism.

Her book touches on many aspects of Ghanaian life, history and culture including Pre-Independence processes; the economy; education; its music, dance, markets, festivals, customs and daily life. Due to its variety, it is suitable as a text not only studying about Ghana, but for the African continent in general. It comes complete with an extensive bibliography for all of those who would like to delve deeper into the subject. It will be an excellent tool for researchers, teachers, scholars and students and all who would enlarge their knowledge of African culture. Comprehensive in nature, it can serve as a work book, since each chapter is followed by a set of questions based on the text. A word study list is included at the back of the book for the purpose of enlarging one's vocabulary.

Ghana Under Nkrumah by Christine X Johnson deserves a place in the library of every reputable school, church and university. It is definitely a must in the personal libraries of everyone interested in Africa!

Dr. Margaret T. Burroughs
DuSable Museum of African American History

MAP OF AFRICA

Ghana

COPYRIGHT 1982 THE AFRICAN-AMERICAN INSTITUTE

STATE REGALIA OF GHANA

Reprinted from a souvenir brochure in honor of REPUBLIC DAY, JULY 1, 1960.

THE FLAG OF GHANA

The Flag of Ghana consists of horizontal stripes of red, gold and green with a five-pointed black star in the centre of the gold stripe. the reasons for the choice of colours are as follows:
RED—to commemorate those who worked for independence.
GOLD—to represent the wealth of the country, linked with the old name of the Gold Coast.
DARK GREEN—to represent the forests and farms of the country.
BLACK STAR—the lodestar of African freedom.

GHANA COAT-OF ARMS

The Coat-of-Arms of Ghana consists of a shield divided into four quarters by a green St. George's Cross rimmed with gold. In the top left-hand quarter is a crossed linguist stick and ceremonial sword on a blue background, representing local administration. In the top right-hand quarter is a heraldic castle on a heraldic sea with a light blue background, representing national government. In the bottom two quarters will be found a cocoa tree and a mine shaft representing the wealth of the country.

In the centre of the green St. George's Cross will be found a gold lion, representing the continued link between Ghana and the Commonwealth. Surmounting the shield is a black five-pointed star rimmed with gold, representing the lodestar of African freedom, and this star stands on a wreath of the colours red, gold and green which again stands on the top of the shield. Under the shield will be found the motto FREEDOM and JUSTICE. The supporters of the Coat-of-Arms are two eagles, coloured gold, and round each eagle's neck hangs another black star suspended from a ribbon in Ghana colours.

THE GHANA SWORD OF STATE

The Sword of State is the symbol of Presidential authority. It is held by the President as he takes the Oath of State at his inauguration, and will be borne before him when he comes to the National Assembly for the state opening of Parliament on July 4. It is of solid gold, and its design is based on that of the double-bladed Afena-nta" (the traditional symbol of inter-state peace).

LEFT
The Sword bears on one side the following symbols:
1. "Nyame-tum" (a square, a circle and a triangle, known as God's power"), symbolizing the presence of God in society
2. "Adehye-borobe" (a symbol based on the shape of the pineapple), signifying royalty and sovereignty.

RIGHT
On the other side are the following symbols:
3. "Fawoho" (symbol of freedom)
4. "Bi-nka-bi" (symbol of justice)
5. "Adehye-borobe" (as explained)
Linking the two blades at the top rests the Ghana Star, symbolizing the oneness of the nation as also, the lodestar of African freedom.

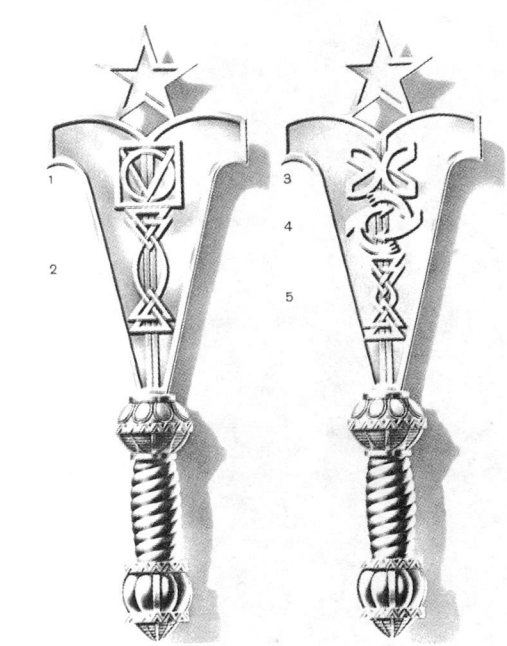

Christine X Johnson

THE PRESIDENT'S PERSONAL STANDARD

This standard consists of the Ghana Presidential Coat-of-Arms on a blue background. The Coat-of-Arms is made up of the Black Star and the flying eagles of Ghana, with the following two traditional symbols:
1. The three concentric circles, "Adinkerahene" (symbol of sovereignty)
2. The cross "Kerapa", otherwise known as "Musuyide" (symbol of good luck and sanctity).

The President's Personal Standard Pole

Inside the President's office his personal standard stands unfurled on a gilded standard pole. This is decorated with the following symbols:

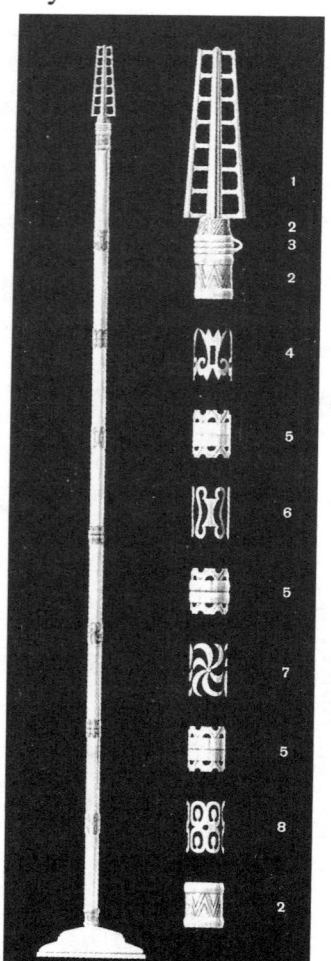

1. "Perekese" (symbol of the personal importance of a sovereign)

2. "Owo-foro-dobe" (symbol of diplomacy and prudence)

3. "Nkonkyema" (symbol of beauty)

4. "Dwantire" (symbol of guiltlessness)

5. "Babadua" (symbol of continuity of life)

6. "Nkonsonkonson" (symbol of human relationship)

7. "Nkyinkyim" (symbol of selfless service)

8. "Ntesie" ["Mate-Masie"], (symbol of wisdom)

The Ghana Mace Symbol of Authority of Parliament

The design of the Ghana Mace is made up of various Ghanaian traditional symbols. They are reading from top to bottom:

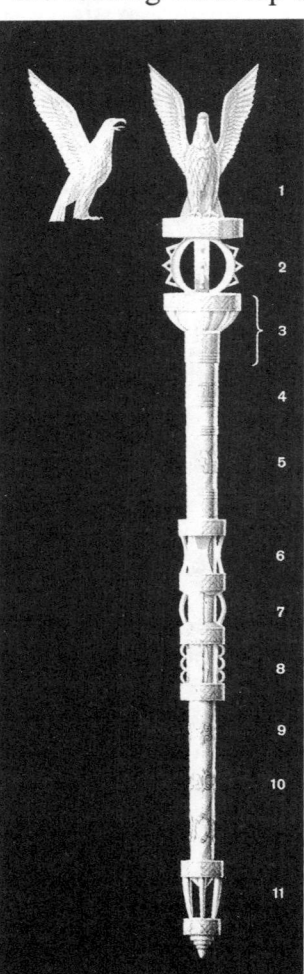

1. The flying eagle (symbolizing the State of Ghana)

2. "Kontonkurawi" (symbol of the common sharing of responsibility)

3. "Nyamedua" (a stool symbol of the presence of God in society)

4. "Hwemdua" (symbol of critical examination)

5. "Gye-Nyame" [except God], (symbol of the omnipotence of God)

6. "Kudu-pono" (symbol of lasting personality)

7. "Mbaadwa" (symbol of the presence and effect of feminine power in society)

8. "Dwanimmen" (symbol of manly strength)

9. "Hye-wo-nhye" [burnt but unburnt], (symbol of imperishability)

10. "Bi-nka-bi" [no one bites another], (symbol of justice)

11. "Kuntunkantan" [bent only to straighten], (symbol of the pride of state)

Ghana Under Nkrumah

STAMPS

Third Anniversary of Independence

Christine X Johnson

xv

LIBATION PRAYER

Grand Spirits of Ghana's Ancestors,
Drink!
Harken, grand Sires,
That God may know
That Ghana is up
To greet
And thank Him.
Great, Dependable God of our Ancestors,
Creator of all, the secret
Of whose design no one can tell;
Whose origin inquisitive
Humanity has since creation
Sought without success to know,
Because no one can know.

Grandfather, Ever-beckoning Grandfather,
To whom the young and old do call,
In joy we call upon Thee this morning;
We crave in humility for grace;
We crave in humility for health;
We crave in humility for progress;
We crave in humility for good fortune;
We crave in humility for long life.

Thou art the thumb
Without which no one can
Make a knot.
Ghana went into consultation,
We went and consulted the *Old Lady*;
And what did she say?
She bade us tell the world
Progress follows after change,
And Ghana must change
From incomplete independence
To become a fully-fledged Republic.

Whereupon the sons of Ghana
Went in search of a leader.
And when to the base
Of the *Stool of Prosperity*
We directed our staffs,
We were told
That wise son Kwame Nkrumah
Is the courageous one
Who with humility
And the fear of God
And the nature of wisdom
Should come to rule the Republic.

First Son of a distant past
That had no creator.
If the Head of State has any power
Then it is the people's will
That has given it to him;
And what people's will has given
The same people's will can reclaim.

Our Great Ancestor
A climber that climbs a good tree
Deserves our aid.
We pray Thee
Be the protector and guide
Of this our Head of State.
If we should wish him anything
We wish him long life;
If we should leave him anything
We leave him a stately walk.
Kwame, go gently!

Grand Spirits of our Ancestors,
Drink!
Give life to the sons of Ghana,
Give life to the Ghana-Guinea union,
Give life to the union of Africa.

Offered on the occasion of the opening of
The First Session of the First Parliament

FOUNDERS OF MODERN GHANA [1]

Dr. Kwame Nkrumah, the Prime Minister, later President of Ghana was educated at Achimoto College, Ghana, at Lincoln University and University of Pennsylvania in the United States and London University in England. As in the British system, the President is the leader of the party in power. He said "Independence comes only once — the Ghanaian Independence will continue to be celebrated in the hearts of her people long after the official celebrations are over. These, however, are not likely to be soon forgotten. And even when the memory itself begins to fade, there will be the tangible symbols of Independence—the flag, the emblem and the state movement—to remind future generations of the achievements and meaning of the past.

That they should be so reminded is important, for it is with these generations, schooled to a new world of freedom, progress and development that Ghana's future ultimately lies."

INDEPENDENCE

When the dawn of independence breaks
Upon this golden shore, oh let it break
Upon a land wherein the beauteous glow
Of liberty has chased away the gloom of
Greed and the clouds of strife.
A land wherein the bitter scrounge of hate
Has long decayed . . .
For bitterness is a blight terrible and sore,
And independence that thrives
In mutual bickering and dislike is servitude
In every land.

So come and abide nor e'er depart
Sweet independence:
But break upon a land made fair
With filial love:
Where tribe with tribe forever dwells
In sweet fraternity.

Der Anang, 1943

[1] *Ghana 1957*, pg. 46.

The Prime Minister, Hon Kwame Nkrumah, LLD, MP (centre, seated), and his cabinet. Full cabinet listing on page 108.

Christine X Johnson

1960, Sister Christine Johnson and Mrs. Nkrumah (right), at a reception in Ghana.

July 1970, Sister Christine Johnson meets with her friend Dr. Kwame Nkrumah in Conakry, Guinea.

Ghana Under Nkrumah

INTRODUCTION

It began in 1937. I received a scholarship from the State of Kentucky to the Universal School of Handicraft and Occupational Therapy, in New York City at Rockefeller Center. Long before the new Negro Rebellion and Social Reconstruction era. It was at the time of the Great Depression, soup lines, unemployment and the Roosevelt era.

One day I went to visit my friend Ruby Owosu, who lived in Harlem and had a husband from Nigeria. Ruby and I were room mates at Meharry Medical College, Hubbard Hospital. Often when I left school in the Rockefeller Center Building on the 25th floor, instead of going to my room at Lincoln Hospital in the Bronx, I would go to Harlem and visit her.

Ruby lived in a large apartment building and at the time there were only a few Africans in New York and most of them worked on the large ships that brought cargo from Africa. Only a few students were around.

Whenever I visited Ruby there would be some of the fellows there and being young and single, they all wanted to date me. Finally I did allow one of the fellows to take me to shows and dances. We were good friends, not serious.

One day when I came by, there was a young man wearing glasses, who was introduced as Kwame Frances Nkrumah, they all called him Frances.

Whenever I came there was a discussion around questions such as "What are the Negroes doing to liberate themselves in America." My defense was to ask the question "Why do you say you have a country, when someone else is running it?" The exchange sometimes got hot and heavy and Ruby would always leave, because she did not want to participate in the discussions. I enjoyed them. They were stimulating and informative to me.

The day I met Nkrumah the conversation drifted to our favorite theme Negro versus African.

Nkrumah was a quiet young man and very serious. As our discussion progressed, he joined in. His voice and mannerisms and what he said made all of us stop and listen. He always said the right things at the right time and it was so profound, we could not argue with him, and as time went by my respect and admiration for his brilliance increased. Even those men who were much older than he, listened with respect and sometimes awe.

In our lighter moments we would dance. He was a very good dancer and he asked to take me out to dance several times. We did go out, but in those days there was no money. Often we walked in the park and ate popcorn and peanuts, because neither of us had the price for a movie. Whenever some

Christine X Johnson

of my friends gave parties, I would invite him, but never to the wild ones. We were more pals than sweethearts.

Finally my term at the Universal School ended and I was given a job in Petersburg, Virginia, through the Nurse's Association, so I left New York to go to Virginia to become an Occupational Therapist at the Petersburg, Virginia Hospital. While there Frances and I corresponded. Then a year later I went back to New York on a visit and we met again. Later I went to Detroit, Michigan and one day received a letter from Frances. He sent me his graduation picture and asked me to come to the commencement. I answered, but could not go, because of money, for the Depression was still on.

I did not hear from him until 1947. I saw in the *Chicago Defender* that there had been some trouble in Grayslake Lane in the Gold Coast, and Nkrumah was to blame. They gave the name of the newspaper in the Gold Coast and Nkrumah was the editor. I wrote to the address and he answered. A year later I saw him on T.V. talking to a group of people. He was still on the theme "Kick the white man out of Africa." It went on this way until he was thrown into jail. But while he was there, he wrote to his buddies outside and carried on his campaign. He was let out of jail and later the Gold Coast was free. When he got Independence he wrote and asked me to come to Ghana for their Independence Celebration. I was going on a trip around the world and had included Africa to be my last stop. So I wrote and told him that I would see him in August since I could not be there in March 1957.

My first impression of Africa was in Nigeria where I first landed. I roamed all over Nigeria, met many friends and finally I got to Ghana. The two people who were with me were skeptical that I knew Nkrumah.

Finally, we met. I hardly knew him after 15 years. He did not now wear glasses, was more mature and handsome. We had much to talk about, old times, and then we made a schedule for movies, dinner and calls on the telephone. I made many pictures while there and when I left Ghana, he sent one of his men to the airport with a gift for me. A gold necklace with an elephant on it.

While in Ghana I met Mrs. Marcus Garvey, who was living in Kumasi, and she drove me to her home where I met Prempi II, who told me of the slavery that led me to my being apart from Ghana and my people.

I was also a good friend of Shirley Graham DuBois and Dr. W.E.B. Dubois while they lived in New York, U.S.A. I used to go to their home for breakfast and luncheon and take my brother Charles Claybourne with me. After they went to Ghana in 1950, I went to visit them. We went for rides in his car given to him by the Russians. The last time I saw Dr. DuBois was two weeks before his death. I continued to go to Ghana and each time I would stop by Shirley's home. Then when she was forced to go to Egypt I went to see her and she and I would go to visit the ancient halls there. When she came to the Bahamas I met her over there and when she came to the United States I was able to see her again. Her death in China was quite a shock. Shirley and I had much in common and were very dear friends.

FROM THE COLD COAST TO GHANA

Ghana — a new Nation—developing modern skills and techniques without losing her African personality and culture.

Ghana — a vigorous Nation-taking great strides in developing its natural and human resources.

Ghana — an exuberant Country, as colorful as the traditional Kente cloth-as melodic as her talking drums and smiling people.

The people of Ghana are believed to have migrated from the ancient empire of Ghana in the North, more than 700 years ago.

Portuguese traders in 1471 were the first Europeans to discover gold, soon the coast was a chain of forts with traders from Portugal, Denmark, Sweden, Britain and Holland. The traders learned that the traffic in human slaves was profitable and continued it for almost 200 years.

In 1844 Britain, which had gained control of the area, signed a Bond of Mutual Cooperation at Cape Coast with the Coastal Chiefs.

The movement for independence reached its peak after World War II under the leadership of Kwame Nkrumah. Arrested for his "Positive Action" Campaign, Dr. Nkrumah was overwhelmingly elected to the then Legislative Assembly in 1951 while still in prison. Summoned from prison by the British Governor, he was asked to form the first Government under the new Constitution. In 1954 he formed the first All-African Cabinet.

Thus began the peaceful process toward complete independence. The assembly launched a Development Plan to improve the spirit and dedication of the Ghanaian people. The British Crown recognized that the people were ready for self government.

"My government in the United Kingdom has ceased from today to have any authority in Ghana," proclaimed the Queen of England through her representative, the Duchess of Kent, only 6 years later.

Independence Day came on March 6, 1957; at the stroke of midnight—Ghana was born. As the solemn ceremonies within the National Assembly were concluded, the shouts of the masses outside, hailed the coming of independence.

The people rejoiced and for days the people in every region celebrated the coming of freedom. Fireworks, parades and dancing, marked the event, jubilation was contagious and the world sent its greetings. And as President Dwight D. Eisenhower said "We are proud that some of your distinguished leaders have been educated in the United States. We are also proud that many of our most accomplished citizens had their ancestry in your country. We are pleased that trade between our two countries has developed to the benefit of both countries. But most importantly, we revere in common with you the great and eternal principles which characterize the free democratic way of life."

Official delegations from 72 countries were present. More than 200 journalist, broadcasters, photographers and T.V. men covered the independence for the newspapers and airwaves of the world. Two days later Ghana was unanimously elected to the United Nations.

Three months later, after independence an African Nation for the first time was represented at the Conference of Commonwealth Prime Ministers in London. Dr. Kwame Nkrumah spoke for his country.

Ghana called a conference of Independent African States in April 1958. This conference stressed the need to assert the African personality in the cause of peace, explored trade possibilities among African States and

Christine X Johnson

called for the end of Colonialism and racism.

Nkrumah taught the people of the Gold Coast that political emancipation from Imperialist domination was a way of existence and not something they did in their spare time. In the schools that existed some students and some teachers had demonstrated against the arrest of some political leaders. The authorities expelled them. This population was distracted at the loss of the new doubly precious education, but Nkrumah proposed the formation of secondary schools independent of the British Colonial Government. A hall was hired in Cape Coast; kerosene packing cases and boards were brought to serve as desks and seats. The expelled teachers became the staff. There were only 10 students to begin with. One year later the school had 240 students, with a thousand students on the waiting list. This was the beginning of a National Education movement. At news of the foundation of the school requests poured in from all over the country. New schools were founded within a few days of each other. A dozen schools and colleges were founded and there were elementary schools in the far areas of Ashanti and Togoland. The people subscribed, chiefs appropriated land, teachers worked for small salaries, and the nation that was to become Ghana sprang into being. To think that Nkrumah merely mobilized the people against the oppression of British Imperialism is to misunderstand one of the great political achievements of our century.

This was the basis of Nkrumah's defeat of British Imperialism. He set the people in motion, discovered and unleashed the immense powers latent in an apparently docile African people. But along with the confidence in and discovery of the power of the people Nkrumah boldly created organizations to unleash and harness political power.

In September 1948, he founded a one-sheet evening papers, the *Accra Evening News*, which became the foundation of the press, which was soon as powerful a means of mobilizing the end of the Gold Coast as education had mobilized the youth. In January 1949 appeared a daily *Morning Telegraph* of Sekondi, followed by another daily, The *Daily Mail* of Cape Coast. These papers attained a fabulous reputation. The *Evening News* sold all the copies it could print. It was besieged by news vendors and the editors of those days claimed that if they had the facilities to print they would have sold 50,000 copies a day in Accra, a town of 150,000 people of whom a large proportion was illiterate. Copies were passed from hand to hand.

This was the way Nkrumah mobilized the people of the Gold Coast against British Imperialism. This was the birth of African Freedom. The people of the Gold Coast became a Nation, and the Nation had won its Freedom. The British Government did not give or grant anything. It was helpless before the new Nation.

It would be dishonorable to attempt to deny that Nkrumah did not establish a viable regime in Ghana. There are points when he laid down lines which future states would follow. There are others in which he failed.

There, however, are only two points to be made; First, a long line of historical events, or failures of African-States, show that Nkrumah's failure was not a failure of individual personality. It was the impossibility of establishing a viable regime and bringing some order to the masses that the imperialists had left behind. Second, what is astonishing is not the failure but the successes. When have so many millions moved so far and so fast?

To Africans, and peoples of African descent everywhere, the name of Nkrumah became for many years a symbol of release from the subordination to which they had been subjected for so many centuries. " After Marcus Garvey there is no other name that is so symbolical of African Freedom as that of Nkrumah." (C.L.R. James, *Black World*, 1972).

Schools were very important to Nkrumah and so Primary and Middle schools were entirely free and compulsory. Parents pay no fee and buy no books. Secondary schools students are also supplied free books. From this you can see the tremendous advance of education in the six or seven years that Ghana has had since its independence.

I was in Ghana in 1957 through 1966. I made many pictures of buildings and other improvements, as positive proof of what the Government was doing for the people. I saw none of the things in the pictures of this book in 1957, and I was all over the country. Mud huts were the order of the day. While the Colonist lived in the big houses with all the trimmings. Today some of the villages have electricity, prefabricated houses, and running water. I made pictures of Tema in 1957, which was a small mud hut fishing village. Today it is a shining city with sidewalks, electricity, pre-fabricated houses with all the modern conveniences, and a population well over 50,000. This proves that the Ghana Government was not spending money on themselves and sending it out of the country. On the contrary the reason they couldn't find any money that Nkrumah had in foreign banks is that he never sent any out of the country to put in there in the first place.

I was in Ghana in 1966 at the opening of the "Volta River Dam", which was to supply water and electric power to the country-side like the "TVA" Tennessee Valley Authority, here in America, and I left the country one week before Nkrumah's over-throw or "Coup". We had discussed his role outside the country on his trip to Vietnam. He felt that since Ho-Chi-Minh was an old friend of his (having met Ho in America during his student days) he should go and see if he could be of service. He also felt that since he had been the target of 13 assassination attempts, that his fate was in hands higher than his. We left it at that. I left Ghana with a feeling that trouble would soon come to him and was not surprised to hear of the "Coup."

I saw Nkrumah in exile in Guinea, West Africa, four years later, a few months before he died. He was in good spirits and eager to return to Ghana. He died in the belief that his beloved country would one day be free. I believed Francis Nkia Kofe Kwame Nkrumah. Of all the many men and women, it had been my good fortune to know, he exemplified the "Rags to Riches and Power" that Horatio Alger wrote about and he is the only Black man that I personally know that became President of his country.

The idea of *Ghana Under Nkrumah*, with historic pictures was conceived after using slides and pictures in classrooms, from Kindergarten through High School, also on lecture tours, since our children and most young men and women grew up in a visual world and visual aids are frequently used in schools, and knowing the limited reading abilities of American youth, I feel that this kind of book would appeal, and demand reader interest for all age groups.

In 1960 while in Ghana at the African and African American World Conference, I attended a party given by Dr. Kwame Nkrumah where he spoke of his plans for Ghana. I knew then this book was necessaryand, and if it inspires some Black boy or girl to do more research and compile a better book for my people, my labor was not in vain.

Christine X Johnson

THE SAGA OF NKRUMAH
Christine X Johnson, May 16, 1972

1
Nkrumah's gone
He died away from home,
An exile, they said
From Africa to Rome.

2
Nkrumah's gone
An exile like me,
Whose ancestors were sent
Across the sea.

3
Never to return
To claim the land
That was taken from me
By a robber band.

4
Nkrumah's gone
Never more to see
The land he reclaimed
For you and me.

5
His relatives and friends
Barred him away
From the land he loved,
And let his enemies stay

6
Don't moan and groan
That's a burden of life
In this world we live
Of sin and strife.

7
Yes, Nkrumah died,
But his deeds will live on,
In the memories of loves ones
Until our lives are gone.

8
Nkrumah's gone,
May his soul rest in peace
He caught hell here on earth
Let persecution cease.

9
His soul was set free,
His destiny fulfilled,
He came here on earth
And did as God willed.

10
So Nkrumah's dead
Why can't he die,
Like DuBois and Malcolm
Yes, like you and I.

11
Yet the world moved on,
From one crisis to another,
Men fighting and dying
And hating each other.

12
Back in the thirties,
When we both were young,
His plans for Africa
Had just begun.

13
He was cold and hungry,
Dejected and scorned,
But he nourished his dreams
Until they were born.

14
I'll go back to Africa
He often would say,
And chase the intruders
Out of Africa to stay.

15
I'll never keep silent
He often would shout
Until Africa is free
And the enemy is out.

16
So back home he went
And put into motion
Political action
Into everyones notion.

17
"Ever forward, backward never"
Was his cry as Ghana was formed.
United and free, we must be
Until African freedom is borned.

18
When all Africa is free
He often would say
United under one Government
That will be the day

19
That Black men,
Wherever they may be,
In Africa, the Islands or USA
Will discover his personality
and see

20
That his dignity and honor
Will make a man,
To stand up and shout,
I'll work for my freedom and
show that I can".

Christine X Johnson

21

Overthrown by traitors
The enemies of men
Who had fought for their freedom
And some were his kin.

22

But another great African.
Who believed in the same
Stepped up and said "come
take refuge in my name".

23

Sekou Toure, an African warrior,
Who had fought for the freedom
Of Guinea from France,
Gave Nkrumah a home and a second
  chance.

24

He realized clearly
That for Africa to be free
He must use all the unity
For others to see.

25

He stepped forth with boldness
When Nkrumah died,
And answered the vultures,
Whose demands he defied.

26

They banned him from Ghana
The country he helped form
And refused him an entry
When he wanted to come home.

27

Nkrumah he said
Will return home again,
If you follow these dictates
And release all his men.

28

Lift restrictions on others
Who wish to come home
Recognize him as President
And honor your own.

29

So Nkrumah's returned
To Ghana at last,
Let's stop all this quarreling
And finish his task.

30

As soon as he died
Came a great hue and cry.
Memorials for Nkrumah
Was heard far and wide.

31

Honor the living
Not the deceased
Stop being a hypocrite
Let this degenerate custom cease.

Ghana Under Nkrumah

STUDY MODULES

AFRICAN VILLAGE COMPOUND [2]

Our forefathers lived in Africa. They killed the wild animals and used their skins for clothes to wear, to make the heads of drums, and also tents to live in. They built homes made of grass, clay and palm leaves. Some of the homes were round in shape and set close together in groups. These homes are called compounds. Most of the people are kin to one another and share their food, services and money. This is called "communal living" and is known to exist in Asia and Africa for many centuries. This communal living is where Russians got their notions on Communism.

[2] Ghana Information, Section Prints. Embassy of Ghana, pg. 12.

QUESTIONS
1. Where did our foreparents live?
2. What did they do with the animals they killed?
3. What were their homes made out of?
4. What is communal living? Describe it.
5. What is a compound? Describe it.

Women working in their villiage compound.

WORDS
Look up in the dictionary and use in a sentence.
1. Palm
2. Shape
3. Compounds
4. Kin
5. Services
6. Communal
7. Existed
8. Centuries
9. Russians
10. Notions

CANDIDATES FOR THE PRESIDENCY [3]

It was in 1957 that I met Dr. Joseph Boakye Danquah. He invited me to his house for dinner. He talked about the presidency. Whether it should be with the educated people of Ghana or with the Convention People's Party. I was not about to get into politics, so I said nothing, because I come from another country.

Arrangements had now been completed for the National Plebiscite in which the people of Ghana would decide the type of constitution under which the country would be governed. Between April 19th and 27th the people were being asked whether or not they wanted the draft Republican Constitution as proposed by the Government and if so, whether they wished Dr. Kwame Nkrumah or Dr. Joseph Boakye Danquah to be the country's first President.

Hundreds of thousands of pamphlets were being distributed throughout the country. Printed in nine languages, they explained the procedure for voting in the plebiscite and set out the proposals for a Republican form of Government.

[3] *Ghana Today*, vol. 4, no. 4, April 13, 1960.

QUESTIONS
1. When did I meet Dr. Danquah?
2. Did I get involved in the political situation? Why not?
3. What were the people asked between April 19th and 27th?
4. What was distributed throughout the country?
5. How many languages were printed?

WORDS

Look up in the dictionary and use in a sentence.

1. Arrangements
2. Plebiscite
3. Constitution
4. Governed
5. Whether
6. Draft
7. Republican
8. Decide
9. Proposed
10. Pamphlets

Dr. Kwame Nkrumah

Dr. Joseph Boakye Danquah

Christine X Johnson

CHRISTIANSBORG CASTLE [4]
ACCRA GHANA, OFFICIAL RESIDENCE OF KWAME NKRUMAH

On the 6th March, 1957, the Gold Coast was declared an Independent State and was renamed Ghana, after one of the ancient Sudanic Empires which flourished between the 4th and 10th centuries.

Christiansborg Castle was the former residence of the Governor of the Gold Coast, and now serves as Government House and Official residence of the Prime Minister. It was here that Francis Nkrumah met his guests. The castle was successively in the possession of the Swedes, and the Danes before coming into British hands in 1850.

As far as the colonial power was concerned, their task was to govern this artificial creation by the introduction of an administration system which would strengthened their position and from which they could continue the exploitation of the human and material resources of the country.

Moreover, a number of educated Africans became less and less satisfied with their opportunities under the colonial regime. The system of indirect rule in the county meant, in practice the administration of the county by British officials and the predominantly illiterate Chiefs, to the total exclusion of the highly educated well-qualified Africans.

But what finally led to the completion of the last phase of this process was the tact and organizing abilities of one of the greatest Africans that was living, Osagyefo Dr. Kwame Nkrumah. It was under his inspiring and enlightened leadership that on the 6th of March 1957 the Gold Coast became the first of the colonies of British Africa to achieve independence under the name of Ghana.

[4] *Ghana at a Glance* pg. 14.

QUESTIONS
1. When did they rename the Gold Coast?
2. What did they name it, and why?
3. Who possessed the castle before the British?
4. What was the colonial power concerned about?
5. What did the system of indirect control mean?

WORDS
Look up in the dictionary and use in a sentence.

1. Guests
2. Residence
3. Rebuilt
4. Relevant
5. Possession
6. Exploitation
7. Colonial
8. Qualified

Christiansborg Castle

SUPREME COURT BUILDING[5]

The Supreme Court is the highest court and also the final Court of Appeals. Its President is the Chief Justice, who is appointed by the President, by an instrument under the Presidential Seal. Other judges of the Supreme Court also are appointed by the President by an instrument under the Public Seal. The power to remove Judges from office is also vested in the President who may so decide in his own right or upon the resolution of the National Assembly supported by the votes of not less than two-thirds of the Members of Parliament and passed on the grounds of a state misdemeanor.

The Supreme Court shall be deemed duly constituted if it comprises three of five Judges; the determination of any question before the Court shall be according to the opinion of the majority of the bench hearing the case. The Supreme Court is the final Court of Appeals for all matters before the courts in Ghana.

QUESTIONS
1. What is the highest court?
2. How was the Chief Justice appointed?
3. Who can remove Judges from office?

[5] *Facts on Ghana*, pg. 27.

WORDS
Look up in the dictionary and use in a sentence.

1. Supreme
2. Appeals
3. Instrument
4. Vested
5. Resolution
6. Misdemeanor
7. Comprises
8. Opinion

The Supreme Court Building

Christine X Johnson

ACCRA - GENERAL ASSEMBLY [6]

The Constitution of the Republic of Ghana says that "there shall be a Parliament consisting of the President and the National Assembly.." The National Assembly at present consists of 198 members of Parliament. Until the General Elections of June 9, 1965, the National Assembly consisted of 114 members of Parliament including 10 women members whose election was specifically provided for by the Representation of the people (women members) act, 1960.

Without distinction of sex, race, religion or political belief, every person who, being by law a citizen of Ghana, has attained the age of 21 years, and is not disqualified by law on grounds of absence, infirmity, of mind, or criminality, shall be entitled to seek election to Parliament.

Members of Parliament (M.P.) are as a rule elected by the people at five yearly general elections, although there is provision for elections when the need arises. The M.P.s in turn elect a Speaker and Deputy Speakers, the latter being themselves members of Parliament. There are currently two Deputy Speakers.

It is the President who summons a new session or program and dissolves the National Assembly, while the Speaker, apart from presiding over and directing the business of the National Assembly, summons meetings after due consultation with the Government.

Each Parliament is divided into annual sessions so that a period of twelve months shall not elapse between any two settings of the assembly.

[6] *Facts on Ghana*, pg. 20.

QUESTIONS
1. What does the Parliament consist of? Why?
2. How many members in the National Assembly?
3. In 1965 how many members were there?
4. What happened in 1969?
5. Who can seek election to Parliament? Why?

WORDS
Look up in the dictionary and use in a sentence.

1. Parliament
2. Consisting
3. National
4. Assembly
5. Provided
6. Disqualify
7. Elected
8. Directing
9. Summons
10. Annual

The General Assembly Building

ACCRA - HOUSE OF PARLIAMENT [7]

Past the Supreme Court and Parliament House is where the base of the statue of Osagyefo the President still offers the supreme advice to freedom movements - "seek ye first the political Kingdom."

Not far away are the ministries, housed in battery-like, two or three storied concrete structures, the bareness is heightened by uncovered concrete flooring, typical of much Ghanaian construction.

Not far away is the carefully protected Bureau of African Affairs, center of Ghana's strong and urgent call for African unity and National freedom, standing across the way from a United Nations Center, symbol of an even greater unity.

[7] *Facts on Ghana*, pg. 21.

QUESTIONS
1. What is the advice of the Freedom Movement?
2. How are the ministries housed?
3. What is the Bureau of African affairs?

WORDS
Look up in the dictionary and use in a sentence.

1. Urgent
2. Bareness
3. Ministries
4. Heightened
5. Concrete
6. Typical

King George V Memorial Hall, Accra, Ghana — the House of Parliament.

Christine X Johnson

THE NATIONAL ASSEMBLY [8]

The National Assembly returns its one-chamber structure and continues to be elected by the people on the basis of universal adult suffrage. There is a general election and, simultaneously a Presidential election, one at least in every five years.

The President dissolves the Assembly before the 5 year period ends, but in doing so he must submit himself for re-election, a provision which ensures that any conflict between the National Assembly and the President will be resolved by the decision of the people.

[8] *Facts Today*, vol. 1, no. 17, October 6, 1957.

QUESTIONS
1. How is the National Assembly structure elected?
2. How long does it take for the Presidential election?
3. What can the President do before the 5 year period?

WORDS
Look up in the dictionary and use in a sentence.

1. Nation	6. Suffrage
2. Chamber	7. Dissolve
3. Structure	8. Simultaneously
4. Continues	9. Assembly
5. Universal	10. Decision

The National Assembly Building

Ghana Under Nkrumah

MR. AKIWUMI
THE SPEAKER OF THE NATIONAL ASSEMBLY [9]

The National Assembly comprises the Speaker, and not less than 104 members, each member representing a constituency (electoral district). In addition to the 104 members representing electoral districts, ten women were in June 1960, elected to the Assembly under the Representation of the People (women members) Act. Qualifications for election: every citizen of Ghana who is 21 and who is not disqualified by law on grounds of absence, infirmity of mind or criminality is entitled to one vote. No one is prohibited from voting on account of sex, race, tribe, religion or political belief.

Setting - The parliamentary year usually coincides with the financial year.

[9] *Ghana Today*, vol. 1, no. 20, November 27, 1957.

QUESTIONS
1. What does the National Assembly comprise?
2. Who was elected in June 1960?
3. Who is entitled to one vote?

WORDS
Look up in the dictionary and use in a sentence.

1. Assembly
2. Representing
3. Constituency
4. Electoral
5. Qualification
6. Absence
7. Infirm
8. Political
9. Prohibited
10. Comprises

Mr. Akiwuki, Speaker of the National Assembly.

Christine X Johnson

AMBASSADOR HOTEL [10]

In Ghana the 100 bed Hotel Ambassador which has vastly improved comforts and facilities available to visiting businessmen and tourists.

But industries without managers and technicians are as "useless as wells without water." Consequently considerable attention has been given in recent years to the training of men and women to these new skills, and technical institutions are opening up in greater force.

[10] *Ghana 1957*, pg. 28.

QUESTIONS
1. How many rooms does the Ambassador Hotel have?
2. What is "useless as wells without water?"
3. What has considerable attention been given to?
4. What is opening up in greater force?

WORDS
Look up in the dictionary and use in a sentence.

1. Vastly
2. Facilities
3. Improved
4. Comforts
5. Industries
6. Consequently
7. Training
8. Skills

Ambassador Hotel, Accra, Ghana

TELEVISION FOR EDUCATION [11]

Ghana Television was born in the mind of President Nkrumah almost immediately after Ghana won her independence. Plans for the television service started in 1959 when the Ghana Government published a white paper approving the recommendations of Mr. R. D. Calhoun and S. R. Kennedy of the Canadian Broadcasting Corporation.

Members of the Ghanaian television staff serve apprenticeships with the best television companies. Mrs. Shirley DuBois served as director of television, and was sent by the Government to make an intensive study of television systems and techniques in Britain, France, Italy, the German Democratic Republic, Czechoslovakia and Japan. She returned home to organize a specifically Ghanaian approach to television and programming.

QUESTIONS

1. How was Ghanaian television born?
2. When did the plan for television start?
3. Where was Mrs. DuBois sent to study?
4. What did she do when she returned.

WORDS

Look up in the dictionary and use in a sentence.

1. Television
2. Immediately
3. Independence
4. Service
5. Published
6. Approving
7. Recommendations
8. Intensive
9. Apprenticeships
10. Techniques

[11] *Ghana Today*, August 11, 1965, pg. 4.

Mrs. Shirley G. DuBois, Director of Television

Mr. Cecil Forde, Chairman of the Board of Directors of the Ghana Broadcasting Corporation

Christine X Johnson

THE IDEA
Ghana Television will be *GHANAIAN*, *AFRICAN* and *SOCIALIST* in Content [12]

GHANAIAN - Because as President Nkrumah said "Television must assist in the Socialist transformation of Ghana." Our aim is to produce programs based on the needs and interests of our people which lift the level of understanding and broaden horizons, which spur patriotism and engender pride. Television will revive the art of our people, bring scientific laboratories into the classrooms of our pupils, heightening the feeling of unity among the groups that make up our nation.

AFRICAN - Because Africa is a geographical entity with a common experience of oppression and exploitation.

Our television will be a weapon in the struggle for African unity. It will be a weapon in Africa's fight against imperialism, Colonialism and Neo-Colonialism. It will resurrect forgotten glories of African history, of African culture. We shall attempt to organize a quick exchange of films with the African countries, and eventually have traveling news units all over Africa, disseminating news of Ghana and televising what is happening in our Sister States.

SOCIALIST - Because our societies have been traditionally socialist and egalitarian, and because we have chosen socialism as the most just and efficient economic system. The socialist outlook will determine our judgment of events not only in Africa, but through the world. We shall oppose economic, political or military oppression of any people, and support the forces of progress against the faces of of reaction.

[12] *Ghana Today*, August 1965.

QUESTIONS
1. What was the idea?
2. What did President Nkrumah say about being Ghanaian?
3. Why Africa?
4. What did President Nkrumah say about socialism?
5. What shall we oppose?

WORDS
Look up in the dictionary and use in a sentence.

1. Socialist
2. Transformation
3. Horizons
4. Patriotism
5. Engender
6. Geographic
7. Entity
8. Egalitarian
9. Imperialism
10. Disseminating

A view of the TV studios in Accra.

READING THE NEWS
ON GHANA TELEVISION [13]

News is usually one of the smaller departments in a T.V. service. But its size belies its importance and the impact it can make on the service by utilizing fully the potential of the medium. Television news in Ghana will be the heir to a long tradition of journalism that goes back to the talking drums which have been used to transmit and receive messages for several hundred years.

Television news has been aptly described as the "the great journalistic adventure of our times." Its advent seems to be the natural culmination of improvements in methods of collection and dissemination of news. These methods have run the range from newspapers printed on modest equipment with limited resources through the rotary machines that print thousands of copies in a matter of hours to broadcasting studios and transmitters, with their capacity for sending news to people on different continents.

[13] *Ghana Television*, pg. 28.

QUESTIONS
1. What is news?
2. How far back does the tradition of journalism go?
3. What are the methods for printing newspapers?

WORDS
Look up in the dictionary and use in a sentence.

1. Departments
2. Service
3. Impact
4. Utilizing
5. Potential
6. Medium
7. Heir
8. Journalism
9. Transmit
10. Culmination

Reading the news on Ghana Television. The ear phones worn by the cameraman enable him to hear instructions from the producer in the control room.

Christine X Johnson

GHANAIAN TECHNICIANS[14]

The Ghanaians who completed their studies abroad returned home to teach their colleagues what they had learned. They work in co-operation with a team of Canadian experts sent to Ghana under the Aid Agreement.

"We have worked on the theory that all members of the television staff must be acquainted with all aspects of television. Thus, every producer has some knowledge of electronics, every newsman knows something about file processing, every script writer has been introduced to the mysteries of microphone booms, lighting, grids and control."

[14] *Ghana Television*, pg. 10.

QUESTIONS

1. What did the Ghanaians do when they completed their studies?
2. What must the T.V. staff be acquainted with?
3. What should every producer know?
4. What was the script writer introduced to?

WORDS

Look up in the dictionary and use in a sentence.

1. Ghanaians
2. Colleague
3. Canadian
4. Theory
5. Acquainted
6. Producers
7. Electronics
8. Newsman
9. Script
10. Microphone

RECORDING. For the sake of convenience, many television programmes are recorded on tape and then rebroadcast at the desired time.

Ghana Television's recording equipment ranks with the best in the world. Above are two of the crack Ghanaian technicians trained in Ghana and abroad.

A DISCUSSION IN AN ACCRA STUDIO [15]

Training at the school is extremely intense. For more than a year, the camera crews have been actively filming major events in Ghana.

The staff, using the camera, controls, mikes and lights of the training studio, have been putting on practical shows under broadcast conditions. The engineers have been dismantling the complex machines and putting them together again. The graphic artists have been drawing maps, charts, buildings and title cards - many of which will be used to go on the air.

[15] *Ghana Television*, pg. 10.

QUESTIONS

1. How is the training at the school?
2. What have the camera crews been doing?
3. What have the engineers been doing?
4. What have the graphic artists been doing?

WORDS

Look up in the dictionary and use in a sentence.

1. Training
2. Extremely
3. Intense
4. Discussion
5. Actually
6. Filming
7. Practice
8. Engineers
9. Dismantling
10. Graphic

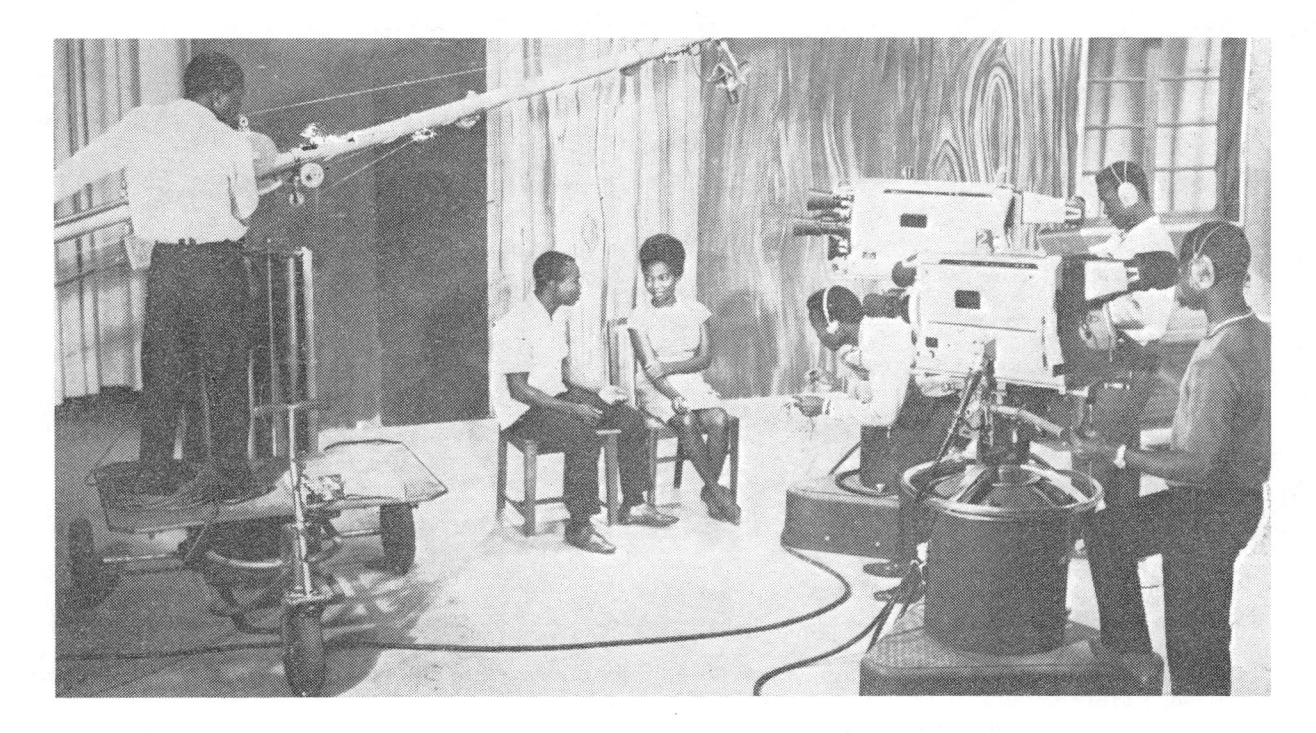

SHOOTING THE PROGRAMME. The essence of television is the programme. Two cameras shoot a panel discussion under a forest of lights in one of the Accra studios. Man on the left is handling a microphone boom, taking care to keep the camera out of the viewer's sight.

Christine X Johnson

GHANA TELEVISION TRAINING SCHOOL [16]

Ghana's advanced T.V. Training school is the first of its kind in Africa, and possibly the world. Under the Aid Agreement with the Canadian Government, many Ghanaians, after completing their basic training at Ghana's T.V. School, were coached under real working conditions in the studios of the Canadian Broadcasting Corporation. For periods from six to fifteen months, they produced shows, edited scripts, handled the cameras, microphones and lights, and assisted in the production of news programs for the Canadian audiences of 10 million viewers. Other Ghanaians studied in the German Democratic Republic, Italy, Great Britain, Japan and Poland.

QUESTIONS

1. What is the first of its kind in Africa?
2. What happened under the Aid Agreement?
3. Where did Ghanaians study?

WORDS

Look up in the dictionary and use in a sentence.

1. Agreement
2. Completing
3. Training
4. Coached
5. Studios
6. Corporation
7. Microphone
8. Assisted
9. Million

[16] *Ghana Today*, vol 9, no. 12, pg. 4.

CLASS. Ghana's Television Training School is unique in Africa. Future personnel receive training in all aspects of television work. The instructor above is giving a lecture on the mysteries of lens focal length and aperture.

AN AUDIO TECHNICIAN [17]

The fact that T.V. is primarily a visual art does not eliminate the need for sound. Below, an audio technician handles the intricate audit console. He makes certain that the microphones are well placed and that the sound is clear and free from static.

What sets Ghana television apart from most of its predecessors is the challenge it has undertaken. The program department of Ghana T.V. will not pursue the capricious Gods of "popularity." Its object will be to serve and not to sell. Its twenty trained and experienced producers and an equal number of production assistants, its writers, announcers and artists will concentrate on a single objective - to educate and edify.

QUESTIONS
1. What is a sound man and what does he do?
2. What sets Ghanaian television apart from its predecessors?
3. What does the program department do?
4. What is its object?

WORDS
Look up in the dictionary and use in a sentence.

1. Primarily   6. Predecessors
2. Eliminate   7. Challenge
3. Technician   8. Department
4. Intricate   9. Capricious
5. Edify   10. Concentrate

[17] *Ghana T.V.*, pg. 24; *Ghana Today*, pg 5.

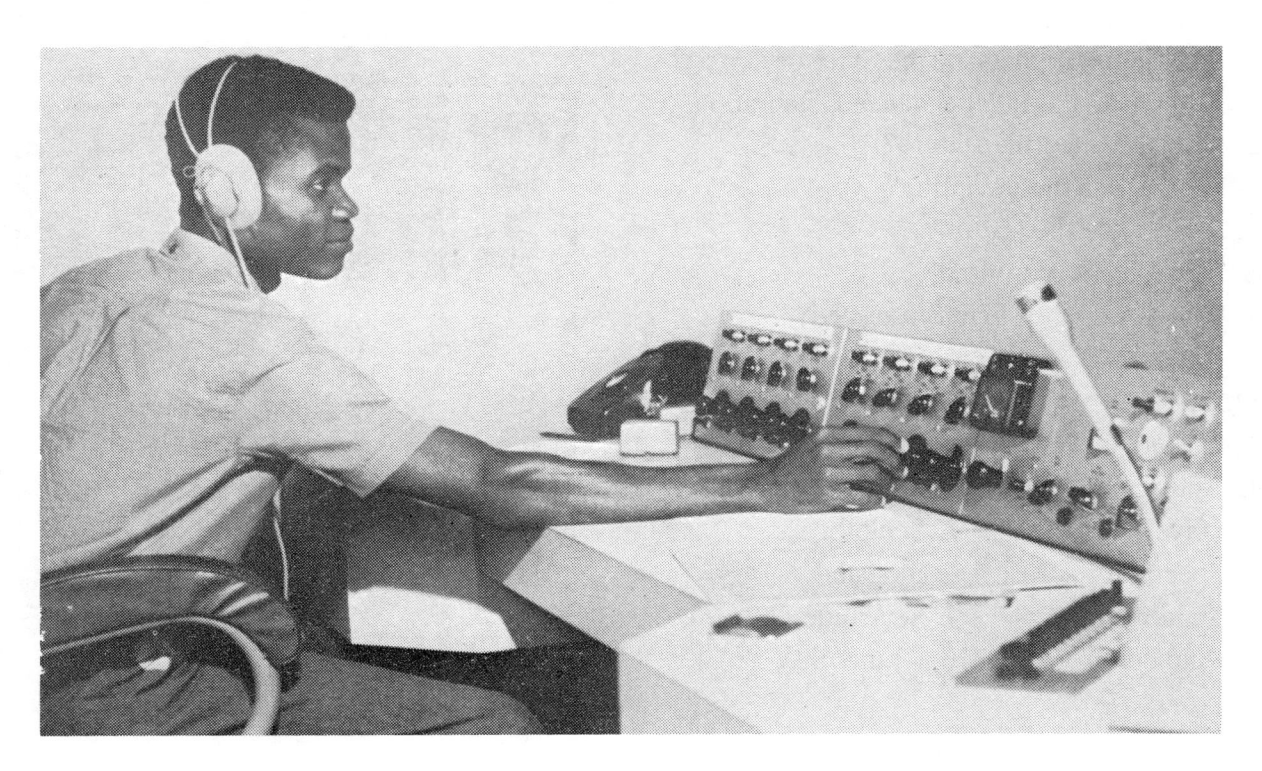

An addio technician handling the audio console. He makes certain that the microphones are well-placed and that the sound is clear and free of static.

STATUE OF KWAME NKRUMAH [18]
FOUNDER OF THE STATE OF GHANA - MARCH 18, 1958

Thousands of spectators gathered at the Ghana Independence Anniversary Celebration to watch the unveiling of the Prime Minister's statue by Chief Justice, Sir Arkin Korsah on the lawn in front of Parliament House. The statue, the work of an Italian Sculptor, Nicola Cadaulla, is one and a half times life size.

Slogans used by Dr. Nkrumah (one of which is "We prefer self government with danger to servitude in tranquility") are inscribed on the sides of the pedestal on which the statue stands.

[18] *Ghana Today*, vol. 2, pgs. 4-5.

QUESTIONS
1. Who is the founder of the State of Ghana?
2. When was the Independence Celebration?
3. Who unveiled the stature?
4. Where was the unveiling?
5. Who made the stature?
6. Name the slogan used?
7. Where was the slogan inscribed?

WORDS
Look up in the dictionary and use in a sentence.

1. Anniversary
2. Unveiling
3. Spectators
4. Statue
5. Founder
6. Slogan
7. Sculptor
8. Slogans
9. Servitude
10. Tranquility

Statue of Kwame Nkrumah, founder of Ghana.

NKRUMAH AVENUE

The bold sweep of Nkrumah Avenue in Accra, runs up perpendicular to the coast line, past Cocoa House, the large modern stores, and the foreign airline offices with their glossy pamphlets.

It now has dual carriage ways and is a very popular street, not like the street under British rule.

QUESTIONS
1. Describe Nkrumah Avenue?
2. What does the avenue run perpendicular to?
3. What do you pass when you travel on Nkrumah Avenue?

WORDS
Look up in the dictionary and use in a sentence.
1. Perpendicular   5. Airline
2. Coast   6. Pamphlet
3. Modern   7. Carriage
4. Foreign   8. Glossy

Nkrumah Avenue, Accra, Ghana.

Christine X Johnson

COCOA [19]
and the COCOA RESEARCH INSTITUTE [20]

In 1951 when the Nkrumah Government took over practical control of the nation from the British, the cocoa crop was endangered by swollen shoot, a disease which destroys the cocoa-bearing trees. The native government waged a vigorous campaign against the disease. The diseased trees were cut out, the others sprayed, and farmers were shown how to prevent the disease from spreading. Today, Ghana's cocoa crop is surpassing all previous records.

The cocoa export tax is the largest single source of revenue. In 1962, Ghana exported 421,227 tons of cocoa over seas, valued at $187,663,900. This represents roughly 40% of the world's total output.

QUESTIONS
1. What is swollen shoot?
2. What did the government do?
3. What happened to the trees?
4. What is the largest source of revenue?
5. How much did Ghana export in 1962?

WORDS

Look up in the dictionary and use in a sentence.

1. Government
2. Practical
3. Control
4. Endangered
5. Swollen
6. Destroy
7. Export
8. Revenue
9. Waged
10. Surpassing

[19] *Ghana Today*, October 16, 1957.
[20] *Ghana Today*, April 13, 1960.

The Cocoa Research Institute in Accra hosts a National Agricultural Show.

COCOA NURSERY [21]

Cocoa is grown by about 300,000 small farmers, many of whom operate farms of a few acres.

The West African Cocoa Research Institute is seeking ways of combating plant disease and improving yield. Results are shared with other African territories. Demonstrations and free advice are given to farmers all over the country, as production is almost completely in the hands of the small scale farmer.

[21] Ghana Information Service, Embassy of Ghana, pg. 21.

QUESTIONS
1. Who is seeking ways of combating plant disease?
2. Who are the results shared with?
3. What do the farmers all over the country receive?

WORDS
Look up in the dictionary and use in a sentence.

1. Operate
2. Farms
3. Acres
4. Yield
5. Research
6. Institute
7. Territories
8. Improving

Cocoa Nursery

COCOA - THE CROP [22]

The crop is produced mostly in the forest belt of Ashanti Brong Ahafo, the Eastern, Western and Central regions. Ashanti accounts for about three fifths of the total supply. There are also large cocoa farms around Ho and between Kpandu and Jasikan in the Volta region.

Improved planting methods and control of the "swollen shoot" disease have accounted for the increased production of cocoa.

[22] *Ghana Today*, Information Section of the Ghana Office, vol. 1, no. 16.

QUESTIONS
1. Where is cocoa produced?
2. How much does Ashanti account for?
3. Where are the other large cocoa farms?
4. What disease does cocoa have?

WORDS
Look up in the dictionary and use in a sentence.
1. Produced   5. Shoot
2. Ashanti   6. Disease
3. Improved   7. Increased
4. Swollen   8. Production

Cocoa, the plant.

GATHERING COCOA IN GHANA [23]

Before independence, Ghana had only a handful of industries. Her economy depended largely on agricultural resources, chiefly cocoa.

Ghana's chief wealth lies in the cocoa crop, which provides over 60% of the value of all Ghana's exports. Ghana is the largest cocoa producer in the world, and the revenue from crop has supplied the Ghanaian Government with funds for roads, schools and hospitals. There is no plantation system in the country; the cocoa trees are owned by about 300,000 small independent farmers.

Some of the important industries include a cocoa processing plant at Takoradi, a cocoa processing and chocolate factory with a capacity of producing 30,000 tons per year.

QUESTIONS
1. Before independence what did Ghana depend on?
2. What were some of the important industries in Ghana?
3. What is the most important industry in the country?
4. Is there a plantation system in Ghana?

WORDS

Look up in the dictionary and use in a sentence.

1. Producer
2. Depended
3. Resources
4. Supplied
5. Plantation
6. Describe
7. Moist
8. Tropical
9. Disease

[23] *Ghana Today*, Information Services, vol.9, no. 14, September 8, 1965.

A young man assists his mother with the cocoa crop.

Christine X Johnson

COMMERCIAL COCOA HARVESTING

The most important commercial crop in the county is cocoa, which has been described as the life-blood of Ghana. As the world's leading producer, Ghana accounts for about one third of the world's total supply.

The tree "Theobroma Cocoa" thrives in a hot moist climate and is well suited to conditions in the tropical rain forest country in Ghana. The tree is reported to have been first introduced into Ghana in 1878 by one Tetteh Quarshie, and it has flourished ever since except for the major set back caused by the swollen shoot disease in recent years.

QUESTIONS
1. What is the important crop in the country?
2. How does the Theobroma Cocoas thrive?
3. Who first introduced cocoa to Ghana?
4. What caused it's set back?

WORDS

Look up in the dictionary and use in a sentence.

1. Commercial   5. Introduced
2. Describe   6. Flourished
3. Produce   7. Except
4. Climate   8. Disease

[24] *Ghana Today*, vol. 1, no. 17, October 16, 1957.

A long extension pole is used to harvest the cocoa high in the tree.

CLIMBING THE PALM TREE
FOR PALM NUTS [25]

This man is climbing the palm tree for palm nuts, which the Ghanaian people make wine from.

The oil palm is an evergreen tree, and is so hardy as to withstand the intense heat caused by farmers burning the bush clearings in readiness for the sowing season. It attains a height of sixty to eighty feet. It has no pith or bark. Its trunk is cylindrical in shape, and devoid of branches; the regular scars found on trees mark the place of pinnate leaves that have decayed and fallen off. When properly trimmed the stumps of the leaves are cut away.

[25] *Gold Coast and Ashanti Reader*, E.J.P. Brown, pg.170.

QUESTIONS
1. What kind of tree is the palm?
2. How hardy is it?
3. How tall does it grow?
4. Describe a palm tree?

WORDS
Look up in the dictionary and use in a sentence.

1. Evergreen
2. Hardy
3. Decayed
4. Properly
5. Trimmed
6. Stumps
7. Sowing
8. Pinnate
9. Cylindrical
10. Devoid

Climbing the palm tree for palm nuts.

Christine X Johnson

UP THE PALM TREE TO TAP FOR WINE [26]

The oil palm is at present the most valuable commercial asset of West Africa. It is a tree of great antiquity, for in the most expensive method of embalming the dead ancient Egyptians used the sap of the tree (that is palm wine) for rinsing the abdomen after the intestines had been extracted through an incision, five inches long, made in the inside of the body.

In fact, the uses of this tree are many, supplying such necessaries as food, drink, clothing, timber for building, light, fuel, a powder similar to Fuller's Earth, drugs, materials for roofing huts and making baskets, mats, fishnets, brooms and ropes.

[26] *Gold Coast and Ashanti Reader*, Book II, E.J.P. Brown, pg. 174.

QUESTIONS
1. What is the most valuable asset in West Africa?
2. How is the palm used in embalming?
3. Who used this method?
4. Name 10 uses of the palm?

WORDS
Look up in the dictionary and use in a sentence.

1. Valuable
2. Commercial
3. Antiquity
4. Embalming
5. Abdomen
6. Intestines
7. Powder
8. Similar

Up the palm tree to tap for palm wine.

HEAD LOAD OF PALM NUTS [27]

Although the oil palm is best known for its commercial products palm oil and palm kernels, it must be borne in mind, when considering it in a West African setting, that it is first and foremost a FOOD CROP. Large quantities of palm oil are consumed locally. While it is difficult to get precise figures there is good reason to believe in Nigeria that more is consumed within the country than is exported.

In Ghana and Sierra Leone, palm oil is also an important article of food. Palm oil, besides contributing to a balanced diet by the provision of vegetable fat, has the added value of being rich in Vitamin A. There is considerable scope for extending the consumption of palm oil throughout the tropics with benefit to the health of the people, and from this point of view alone a proper scientific study of the crop, leading to improved production methods, can be readily justified.

[27] *Gold Coast and Ashanti Reader*, Book II, E.J.P. Brown, pgs. 173-174.

QUESTIONS

1. What is palm oil best known for?
2. What is palm oil?
3. Why is it known best in Ghana and Sierra Leone?
4. What vitamin is it rich in?

WORDS

Look up in the dictionary and use in a sentence.

1. Commercial
2. Kernels
3. Considering
4. Consumed
5. Precise
6. Article
7. Contributing
8. Balanced
9. Provision
10. Consumption

This young woman carries a head load of palm nuts.

Christine X Johnson

THE OIL PALM (ELAEIS GUINEENSIS) [28]

The oil palm is an evergreen tree. On the top is a spreading crown of pinnate leaves, in the center of which is a single bud or shoot, this is the only point where growth takes place. Trees attacked by the beetle-grub (Kobu pl. Aboku) become arrested in their growth and have a stunted appearance. The leaves of the oil palm are very long; several exceed 14 ft.; and their footstalks are armed with stout hooked spikes. The main nerves (Minaba) on the exterior of the pinnas or leaflets are used for brooms, whisks, and so forth; and the exterior of the mibrib or petiole (Mpapa) is cut into strips for basket work. The mpapa are also tied together to make torches, which are found very serviceable, if not indispensable while traveling through the bush at night.

QUESTIONS

1. What is an oil palm?
2. What is the shape of its trunk?
3. What is on the top?
4. What are the trees attacked by?
5. How long are the leaves of the palm?
6. What are the leaflets used for?
7. What is the mpapa used for?

WORDS

Look up in the dictionary and use in a sentence.

1. Palm
2. Intense
3. Burning
4. Height
5. Bark
6. Cylindrical
7. Devoid
8. Pinnate
9. Footstalks
10. Whisks

[28] *Gold Coast and Ashanti Reader*, Book II, pgs. 173-174.

The oil palm (Elaeis guineensis.)

PALM OIL FRUIT [29]

In the internal variations of the fruit, a number of different "forms" are recognized. This is of great practical importance, as a study of the inheritance of the various forms is the basis of the breeding program for the improvement of the oil palm.

When seen in section, either longitudnal or transverse, an oil palm fruit shows the following major components: (1) an outer layer, comprising the oily pulp called Mesocarp; (2) an intermediate layer, the hard woolly shell of the nut, surrounding the kernel; and (3) the central kernel.

It is the mesocarp which gives palm oil commerce, while palm kernels are obtained from the central part of the fruit.

The proportions of mesocarp, shell, and kernel vary considerably, and it is these variations which determine the forms into which palm fruits are classified. By far the commonest is the shelled or dura. As its name implies this form is characterized by a thick shell; it has a very thin mesocarp but a large kernel. It will be evident that palms of this form cannot produce a great deal of palm oil, but their kernel production is high. Sometimes oil is expressed from the kernels for making soap. Most of the wild palms in West Africa are of this type.

[29] West African Institute for Oil Palm Research, pg. 13.

QUESTIONS
1. When seen in sections, what are the 3 major components?
2. What gives palm oil commerce?
3. How are the palm fruits classified?
4. How are the palms in West Africa classified?

WORDS
Look up in the dictionary and use in a sentence.

1. Variations
2. Practical
3. Inheritance
4. Breeding
5. Improvement
6. Longitudinal
7. Components
8. Comprising
9. Kernel
10. Recognize

A typical bunch of oil palm fruit.

Christine X Johnson

OIL PALM FRUIT TYPES [30]

UNRIPE   RIPE

1. **Ordinary** - the fruit is black most of the time, but it assumes (nigrescens) a reddish color, which spreads from the top downwards, just before ripening. The great majority of the palm oil met with in the wild state in West Africa are of this type.

2. **Green** (visescens) - the next type, which although reasonably well known, the "green fruited" type occurs only occasionally. The fruit of this type is green until just before ripening when it assumes a brick-red color, which again spreads from the top downwards, then being easy to distinguish from the crimson red of the ordinary type.

3. **Mantled** (poissom) - a third type, which is vary rare in nature, is the "mantled," know botanically as Poissoni. This is distinguished by having a ring or "mantle" of fleshy out growths surrounding the main part of the fruit.

4. **White** (albescens) - which is of some importance but which is exceedingly rare in nature, is the "white fruited" or albescenes. In this type, the oil in the pulp is almost devoid of carotene so that it assumes a whitish tinge which is noticeable to some extent on the outside of the fruit as it ripens.

[30] West African Institute for Oil Palm Research, pg. 13.

QUESTIONS

1. Name the four types of fruit?
2. What color is the first fruit most of the time? Describe it.
3. What color is the second type of fruit? Describe it.
4. Describe the third type.
5. Describe the fourth type.

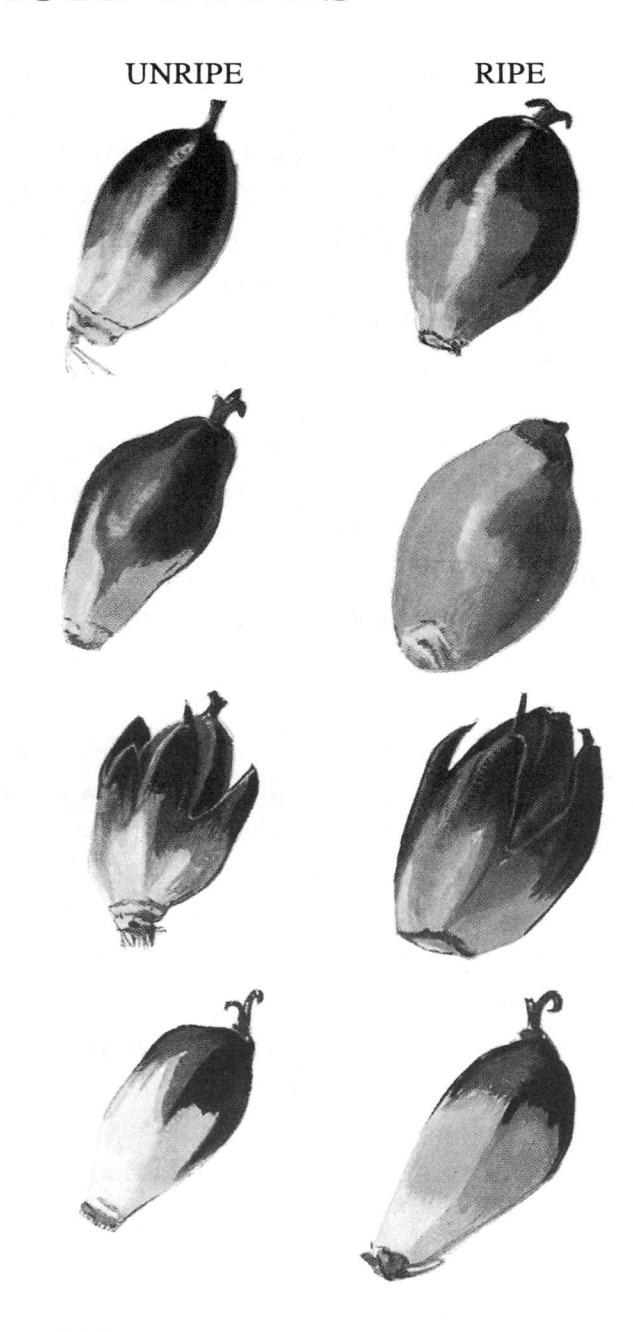

WORDS

Look up in the dictionary and use in a sentence.

1. Assume
2. Majority
3. Mantled
4. Distinguished
5. Carotene
6. Crimson
7. Pulp
8. Devoid

Ghana Under Nkrumah

GHANA YOUNG PIONEERS [31]

Founded in June 1960 these youth organizations aim at inculcating in the youth Ghanaian folklore, culture, and traditions as a means of instilling in them the spirit of leadership and patriotism. Lessons in agriculture and such technical skills, as road building, radio mechanic and music are given to the members.

Membership of the organization is open to all school children between the ages of eight and twenty-two.

[31] *Ghana at a Glance*, pg. 68.

QUESTIONS
1. When was the youth organization founded?
2. What was its aim?
3. What lessons did it give?
4. What age could children belong?

WORDS
Look up in the dictionary and use in a sentence.

1. Founded
2. Organization
3. Inculcating
4. Folklore
5. Culture
6. Leadership
7. Patriot
8. Tradition

Ghana Young Pioneers, 1962.

Christine X Johnson

COMMUNITY CENTER [32]

The majority of Ghanaians are agricultural workers who live on farms or in small villages. The Community Center plays a very important role in the lives of the people of Ghana. This is a Community Center in Accra, the capital and principal city of Ghana. The visitors are told the meaning of the "caption" to the picture in front of the center written in the Ga language: "See how nice it is for brothers and sisters to live together." This inscription explains our family life in Ghana.

QUESTIONS
1. What does the caption in the picture say?
2. What language is it in?
3. What does the inscription explain?

WORDS
Look up in the dictionary and use in a sentence.

1. Community
2. Accra
3. Ga
4. Inscription
5. Family
6. Together

[32] *Ghana Today*, vol. 6, no. 5, May 9, 1964.

Community Center in Accra.

Ghana Under Nkrumah

COMMUNITY DEVELOPMENT - GHANA

Here the woman are carrying dirt on their heads to clear a section for a new development of homes.

4,000 houses are to be built at Tema. President Nkrumah has directed that 4,000 more dwelling units be built at Tema by the Tema Development Corporation to meet the increasing demands for accommodations by the workers of the township.

[33] *Ghana Today*, vol. 2, no. 4, pg. 16, 1958.

QUESTIONS

1. How many houses are to be built?
2. Why are they being built?

WORDS

Look up in the dictionary and use in a sentence.

1. Carrying	5. Directed
2. Section	6. Dwellings
3. Houses	7. Increasing
4. Build	8. Demands

The women are skilled at balancing heavy loads of dirt on their heads.

Christine X Johnson

SOCIAL WELFARE
COMMUNITY DEVELOPMENT [34]

This man is holding a large lump of earth in his hands and others are looking at him. The land is what people are thinking, "this is our land and we are proud" we will develop and build upon this land.

The vastly improved standards of living in the rural areas and the growing civic responsibility of the people of Ghana reflect the valuable work of the Department of Social Welfare and Community Development. Although it is a new development, it is firmly established.

QUESTIONS
1. What does the man hold in his hand?
2. What do the people think of the land?
3. What is firmly established?

WORDS
Look up in the dictionary and use in a sentence.

1. Develop
2. Civic
3. Responsibility
4. Welfare
5. Firmly
6. Land
7. Department
8. Established

[34] *Ghana Today*, vol. 2, no. 4, pg. 4.

The people of Ghana have great pride in their land and are working hard to make the Community Development plan a success.

WOMEN IN COMMUNITY DEVELOPMENT [35]

Women carry dirt on their heads as they labor in the community. With babies on their backs the women work as well as men. They are building a community center for everyone.

Rural Training Centers are operated by the Department in each region of the country and are assisted in raising the standard of village life by teaching it's leaders in all aspects of community development and the general principles of village improvement. It is the policy of the Government of Ghana to speed up the economic and social development of the rural areas and to rely as much as possible on the principle of self help in doing so.

QUESTIONS

1. What are women carrying on their heads?
2. What are they building?
3. How are the rural centers operated?
4. What does the Government rely upon?

WORDS

Look up in the dictionary and use in a sentence.

1. Community
2. Building
3. Center
4. Rural
5. Assisted
6. Development
7. Improvement
8. Economic
9. Social
10. Principal

[35] *Ghana Today*, April 16, 1958, pg. 4.

Women are essential to the community and its development.

Christine X Johnson

IMPROVEMENT AND SELF HELP [36]
COMMUNITY DEVELOPMENT — GHANA

Here in the forest trees are being cleared and a chief with an umbrella over him instructs the men and women what to do.

The work of improvement being carried out through self-help in Ghana has attracted visitors from all over the world. Ghana now has an international reputation for its community development programme. Persons from other countries have been sent to study the programme and to receive training in new methods of community development.

[36] *Ghana Today*, Information Services, vol. 2, no. 4, April 16, 1958.

QUESTIONS
1. How is the improvement being carried out?
2. What has Ghana got a reputation for?
3. What have persons from other countries being sent for?

WORDS
Look up in the dictionary and use in a sentence.

1. Forest
2. Cleared
3. Chief
4. Instruct
5. Improvement
6. International
7. Programme
8. Receive
9. Methods
10. Training

The workers clearing the land depend on their chief for leadership.

HEALTH CENTERS [37]
COMMUNITY DEVELOPMENT — GHANA

The earth is carried away in buckets as the man loads a bucket full of dirt and everyone looks happy. The women do their share of carrying the dirt away.

Health centers have been built at selected points. The vastly improved standard of living in the rural areas and the growing civic responsibility of the people of Ghana reflect the valuable work of the Department of Social Welfare and Community Development. Although it is comparatively new development it is very firmly established and its officers can be seen at work in all parts of the country from the large urban centers to the smaller towns and villages.

QUESTIONS

1. How is the earth being carried away?
2. What do the women do?
3. What reflects valuable work?

WORDS

Look up in the dictionary and use in a sentence.

1. Earth
2. Buckets
3. Dirt
4. Health
5. Centers
6. Vastly
7. Standards
8. Comparative
9. Officers
10. Firmly

[37] *Ghana Today*, vol. 2, no. 4, 1958.

The entire community lends a hand.

Christine X Johnson

HOUSING PROJECTS
COMMUNITY DEVELOPMENT - GHANA

The chief is standing under the umbrella here, while the men clear up the field and get the work started on a housing project.

This is a government-sponsored scheme that has been started by which the population in the Frafra and Zuarungu districts are being gradually resettled in Damongo in the Gonja District under a project officially known as the "Frafra Land Resettlement Scheme." It is hoped that once confidence has been established in the project settlement will proceed more rapidly.

[38] *Ghana Today*, vol. 1, no. 20, pg. 3.

QUESTIONS
1. What is the chief doing?
2. What kind of project is this?
3. What districts are involved in the project?
4. What is the project known as?

WORDS
Look up in the dictionary and use in a sentence.

1. District
2. Sponsored
3. Gradually
4. Resettled
5. Confidence
6. Scheme
7. Established
8. Rapidly
9. Government
10. Project

The chiefs presence gives the community more confidence in the new housing project.

SEWERS - COMMUNITY DEVELOPMENT

In Nkrumah's Ghana all kinds of development went along. The making of homes, laying of sewers (shown here in the picture), were signs of the times. Before Independence Ghana (Gold Coast) did not have sewers, running water or electric lights.

There were no thoroughfares, no asphalt streets, or the many things you can now find.

[39] *Ghana Today*, Information Services, vol. 3, no. 5, April 22, 1958.

QUESTIONS
1. What happened to Nkrumah's Ghana?
2. What was it like before Independence?
3. Were the people doing well?

WORDS
Look up in the dictionary and use in a sentence.

1. Development	5. Water
2. Sewers	6. Making
3. Electric	7. Kinds
4. Independence	8. Homes

Laying a sewer by hand is hard work, but everyone is willing to help.

Christine X Johnson

DIGGING WITH HANDS [40]
COMMUNITY DEVELOPMENT - GHANA

In this land of sunshine the people are digging for a sewer. Their hands are what they are digging with, because their colonial masters did not provide them with digging tools.

Without fancy tools they all jump in and share the joy of working. It is important to have a job to do, and to do that job well. They are proud to see and show the results of their hard work. Men, woman and children, all share in the work. This is how Ghana is taking shape.

QUESTIONS
1. What are the people digging for?
2. What do they use?
3. Why are they digging?
4. Who shares in the work?

WORDS
Look up in the dictionary and use in a sentence.

1. People
2. Digging
3. Sewer
4. Produce
5. Share
6. Shape

[40] *Ghana Today*, Information Services, vol. 3, no. 5, April 22, 1958.

Working without tools because there are none, the people in this community dig with their hands.

THE OLD AND THE NEW TEMA HARBOR [41]

Few things in life are ideal and Tema possessed several drawbacks. The chief of these lay in the fact that this was no uninhibited stretch of the coast, but the home of some 4,000 or more Ga-speaking people whose ancestors had lived there for more than two generations before the battle of Katamanso; that is, in the early 18th century. Moreover, then people depended very largely on fishing for their livelihood and their fishing beach lay well within the confines suggested for the new harbor. Clearly the new project would involve considerable disruption of their lives.

A harbor implies a town. For the first time in West Africa, a community could be built up enjoying all of the advantages of modern civilization. Well designed houses, a well equipped hospital and comprehensive health and cultural services, piped water supplies and underground sewerage, planned and lighted streets, well laid out stores and markets, pleasant gardens and open spaces, well equipped schools and community centers. It is a well balanced community in which a variety of industries quite apart from the harbor would be encouraged to provide as many types of employment for the towns people as possible.

Food for the town is provided by developing the agricultural potentiality of the surrounding district through irrigation and the planting of new crops, and the fishing industry, the traditional occupation of the people of Tema, would be similarly encouraged.

The new Tema Harbor.

[41] *The Making of Ghana*, 1965, pg. 28.

THE OLD AND THE NEW TEMA HARBOR

QUESTIONS
1. Was this coast inhabited?
2. Whose ansestors built a town?
3. How many generations before the battle of Katamanso?
4. What did the people depend on?
5. Did the project disrupt their lives?
6. What happened for the first time in West Africa?
7. Describe Tema.
8. Was it well balanced?
9. How is food for the town provided?
10. What was the traditional occupation of Tema?

WORDS
Look up in the dictionary and use in a sentence.

1. Stretch
2. Depended
3. Livelihood
4. Confines
5. Disruption
6. Implies
7. Modern
8. Equipped
9. Balanced
10. Provide

A street in new Tema.

The old fishing village demolished in 1959 after its inhabitants had been resettled some two miles away.

FISHING IN TEMA [42]

So much had been achieved by September 1954. From a small fishing community, more or less self contained apart from the lorry-loads of fish sent to Accra, Tema had been opened up ready for construction to proceed on the harbor proper. Admittedly conditions of living and working would not be ideal at first; the cinemas, restaurants, bars and stores of today's Tema were still things of the future; but they would be luxury itself compared with the experiences of the early pioneers who had prepared the way.

There remain the people who have worked on Tema Harbor, some 3,500 of them when construction was at its peak in 1958. Many nations have come together here, but Ghana has provided, as Ghana should, the core of effort round which all this activity has revolved and it should be a rare day indeed when the cry "Twoo-bo-ee" the traditional chant of the fisherman urging their canoes through the surf, failed to be heard in Tema.

[42] *Tema*, pg. 10.

QUESTIONS
1. How much had been achieved by September 1954?
2. What would be luxury?
3. What did they send to Accra?
4. Who worked on Tema Harbor?
5. When was the peak of construction?
6. What is Twoo-bo-ee?

WORDS
Look up in the dictionary and use in a sentence.

1. Achieved
2. Community
3. Contained
4. Construction
5. Admitted
6. Cinema
7. Future
8. Luxury
9. Compared
10. Experiences

1957, fishermen gathering nets at the end of a day in old Tema.

On September 27, 1958 Dr. Nkrumah placed into position the last block of quay no 2 on the Volta River project. Here he is posing with the divers who guided the block under water.

Christine X Johnson

COMMUNITY CENTER IN TEMA [43]

Working mothers, market women, housewives and all women of the city of Tema attend the community center for recreation classes.

In 1951 the Legislative Assembly approved a more ambitious plan for mass literacy and education. Its essentials were an attack on illiteracy, increased facilities for training in village betterment and increased momentum in all forms of community development.

Between 1952 and 1954, 265,770 learners enrolled in classes; and 66,950 literacy certificates were issued. The vernacular Literature Board continued to produce primers and readers, and to provide general reading matter on which people could exercise their new found powers; five vernacular newspapers were produced with an average circulation of 55,000.

We all sang together. I (the author) am standing in the center, singing with my African sisters.

[43] *The Making of Ghana*, 1965, pg. 30.

QUESTIONS
1. Who comes to the community center for recreation classes?
2. What was approved in 1951?
3. What was its essentials?
4. Between 1952 and 1954, how many learners enrolled?
5. How many vernacular newspapers were produced?

WORDS
Look up in the dictionary and use in a sentence.

1. Market
2. Community
3. Recreation
4. Recruiting
5. Facilities
6. Essential
7. Produced
8. Exercise
9. Vernacular
10. Circulation

Standing center is Christine X Johnson, singing with her African sisters.

USE OF PRIMITIVE METHODS
IN COMMUNITY DEVELOPMENT - GHANA [44]

The hole grows deeper as they pull the dirt up. Scenes like this, the new generation of people in the U.S.A. do not know about, but primitive methods must be used until they can get the tools to work with. This site is being built for a community center.

The work of improvement being carried out through self help in Ghana has attracted visitors from all over the world, and Ghana now has an international reputation for its Community Development Programme.

[44] *Ghana Today*, vol. 2, no. 4, pg. 4.

QUESTIONS
1. What primitive methods are used in Ghana?
2. What will the site be used for?
3. What do visitors from all over the world come to see?

WORDS
Look up in the dictionary and use in a sentence.
1. Generation
2. Primitive
3. Improvement
4. Attractive
5. Visitors
6. World
7. International
8. Reputation

The workers are pulling the dirt preparing to build a community center.

Christine X Johnson

CONSTRUCTION IN TEMA HARBOR [45]

There were 17 interpreter experts plumbing the depths including Europeans, managers recruited from Japan and Ghanaians who had been specially trained on the site.

After preparing the wall's foundations, their job was to mark with the air bubbles from their apparatus the place where each block should go, wait for the derrick driver above to lower his load, then as they felt the block descending on course, to move quickly aside. Not an enviable role and one in which the cliche "slow but sure" would seem to have a new, and vital significance. In fact, the wall was built in record time - 3,250 ft. twenty-six to thirty feet high, in twelve months at a rate of up to 125 blocks a week. Once again completion called for a special ceremony at which the President of Ghana, Dr. Kwame Nkrumah, placed the last block in position. See photo, page 51.

[45] *Tema*, pg. 20.

QUESTIONS
1. What happened after preparing the wall's foundation?
2. How soon was the wall built?
3. How many blocks a week?
4. Who placed the last block in position?

WORDS
Look up in the dictionary and use in a sentence.

1. Construction
2. Interpreter
3. Especially
4. Apparatus
5. Derrick
6. Enviable
7. Role
8. Completion
9. Ceremony
10. Position

A construction worker at Tema Harbor.

HOUSING IN TEMA - FISHING VILLAGE [46]

Economically, the main problem was to strike a balance between the high standards of housing and services and the relatively low incomes of the majority of the towns people. Eighty percent of the population would require dwellings costing less than $200 a room, but they would also need space for the multitude of domestic activities which are, by custom, performed in the open. As a result, though the relatively high site development costs would require a high proportion of single story structures.

Most of Ghana's traditional materials are transients, such as thatch and swish, and a new architecture would have to be converted to conform with the availability and cost of imported materials, while taking full advantage of local materials, the whole project had to be related again to the habits, customs and incomes of the people.

[46] *Tema*, pg. 28.

QUESTIONS
1. What did the government try to strike a balance between?
2. How was most of the domestic activities performed?
3. What were Ghana's traditional building materials?

WORDS
Look up in the dictionary and use in a sentence.

1. Economically
2. Balance
3. Relatively
4. Majority
5. Population
6. Dwelling
7. Require
8. Densities
9. Construction
10. Traditional

Housing in Tema fishing villiage.

Some of the two-story flats in community no 1.

Christine X Johnson

TEMA SAILING CLUB [47]

It is not only private people who benefit from these extensive public works, but also the industries which are essential to the projects final success. In the United States, Ghana's story is being told in continuing meetings between representatives from Ghana and American leaders, in contrast with civic groups, in friendly discussions between Ghana students and their American hosts, and by the printed word-all leading to increasing understanding between the two nations.

[47] *Tema*, pg. 35; *Ghana*, pg. 30.

QUESTIONS
1. Who benefits from the public works?
2. How is Ghana's story being told?

WORDS
Look up in the dictionary and use in a sentence.

1. Private	6. Leaders
2. Extensive	7. Contrast
3. Public	8. Students
4. Industries	9. Hosts
5. Success	10. Nations

Tema Sailing Club situated within the main harbor.

EDUCATIONAL POLICY [48]

Control of educational policy and development passed into African hands not at independence in 1957 but in 1951 when the country achieved a considerable measure of internal self-government. It was in 1951 that the infant-junior schools were renamed primary schools and offered part or all of a 6 year course; the primary schools renamed middle schools offered a 4 year course.

Today, Ghana has one of the highest educational levels in Africa. Ghana spends more on education in relation to her national income than any other country in the world.

[48] *Facts on Ghana*, pg. 32.

QUESTIONS
1. In what year did Africans gain control of the educational system?
2. When was Independence achieved?
3. What are the infant-junior schools now called?
4. What are the primary schools called?

WORDS
Look up in the dictionary and use in a sentence.

1. Infant
2. Education
3. Junior
4. Independence
5. Achieved
6. Income
7. Spend
8. Control
9. Rename
10. Internal

Schoolboys are much the same everywhere.

Christine X Johnson

THE CHIEF'S SCHOOL

A lot of the schools were private. This is one of the Chief's schools. the pupils began their schooling at an early age, 3 or 4. During this course they are taught in their own language. They did not all go to the Missionary schools. They also were taught their own history.

The buildings of the Primary or home schools vary in the form from the dried earth with thatch roofs to outside air.

They learn the basic things in their culture like drumming, and traditional ceremonies.

QUESTIONS

1. Did all children go to the Missionary schools?
2. What did they learn?
3. What language were they taught?
4. Did they learn to drum?

WORDS

Look up in the dictionary and use in a sentence.

1. Pupils
2. Taught
3. Type
4. Thatch
5. Culture
6. Speech
7. Primary
8. Dried
9. Roof
10. Method

Private school belonging to a Chief.

PRIMARY SCHOOLING [49]

The pupils of Ghana begin their schooling when they are between 5 and 6 years of age. During this course they are taught in their own speech, and then for 6 years they attend an Infant-Junior school and follow the basic primary course. But during the second three years of course they learn also to read and write in English. The course aims at producing young people who have a mastery of the "tool subjects" at an elementary level, a basic general knowledge and the ability to think for themselves. From the Infant-Junior schools a select number of the elder pupils pass on to the Senior Primary schools, where they continue their education for another four years beyond the basic course, being taught during these years in English.

The buildings of the Primary schools vary in type from the dried earth, with thatched roofs, which cost little to build, to large double story buildings, built of stone or concrete, which will last for many generations. The average Village Primary school is a single storied building made of concrete blocks, burnt or cut stone. The school has a pleasant compound, with shade trees and flower beds, and neat borders of shrubs edging the paths of the school buildings. There will be one or more playground where football is played all the year round, and a school garden, tended by the children, in which such crops as yams, maize, groundnuts and vegetables will be growing.

[49] *Achievements in the Gold Coast* - Part One.

QUESTIONS
1. At what age do the children of Ghana begin their schooling?
2. At what age do they attend the Infant-Junior school?
3. What speech are they taught in?
4. Why do they learn to read and write in English?
5. Describe the Primary school buildings and their compound?

WORDS
Look up in the dictionary and use in a sentence.

1. Infant
2. Taught
3. Knowledge
4. Education
5. Compound
6. Primary
7. English
8. Producing
9. Vary
10. Generations

A typical Primary school.

Christine X Johnson

SECONDARY SCHOOLS [50]

In 1957 when Ghana became independent there were 571,580 pupils in Primary schools and Middle schools; in 1963-64 the enrollment was over 1.3 million. In the Secondary or High school sector, there were 38 schools with 9,860 pupils in 1957; in 1963-64 the number of Secondary schools increased to 89 with a total enrollment of 32,000. Teacher Training and Technical Education has also increased more than four fold from 1957 to 1963-64.

Elementary education will begin at the age of five and end at the age of twelve.

On finishing the Elementary school course, children will proceed by selection examination at the age of 13 to a Secondary school; then on to a Teacher Training College, a vocational school, or a technical school.

QUESTIONS
1. How many pupils were in Primary and Middle schools in 1957?
2. How many in 1963-64?
3. How much did the Secondary schools increase in 1963-64?
4. At what age does the primary education begin?

WORDS
Look up in the dictionary and use in a sentence.
1. Independent
2. Primary
3. Middle
4. Enrollment
5. Pupils
6. Increased
7. Technical
8. Elementary
9. Selection
10. Examination

[50] *Ghana Today*, no. 1, March 1, 1962, pg. 5.

A Secondary School for children 13 and older.

SECONDARY BOYS SCHOOL [51]

Under colonial rule little attention was paid to education in the Gold Coast, with the result that there was only five percent literacy when Ghanaians achieved independence in 1957. The first major step ever taken to extend the benefits of education to the people of Ghana was in 1951 when the first all African Legislative Assembly was appointed. In that year the Government introduced an accelerated development plan for education which went into effect in January 1952.

The scheme provided a six year basic course of fee-free primary education for every school age child and aimed at hastening the "Africanization" of public life by providing secondary and higher education facilities. It included teacher-training and technical education. Its implementation brought phenomenal expansion to the educational system in the years which followed.

[51] *Facts on Ghana*, pg. 32.

QUESTIONS
1. What happened under colonial rule?
2. What was the former name of Ghana?
3. What happened when the all African Legislature was appointed?
4. What did the scheme provide?

WORDS
Look up in the dictionary and use in a sentence.

1. Literary
2. Achieved
3. Major
4. Extend
5. Accelerate
6. Introduced
7. Effect
8. Provided
9. Facilities
10. Implementation

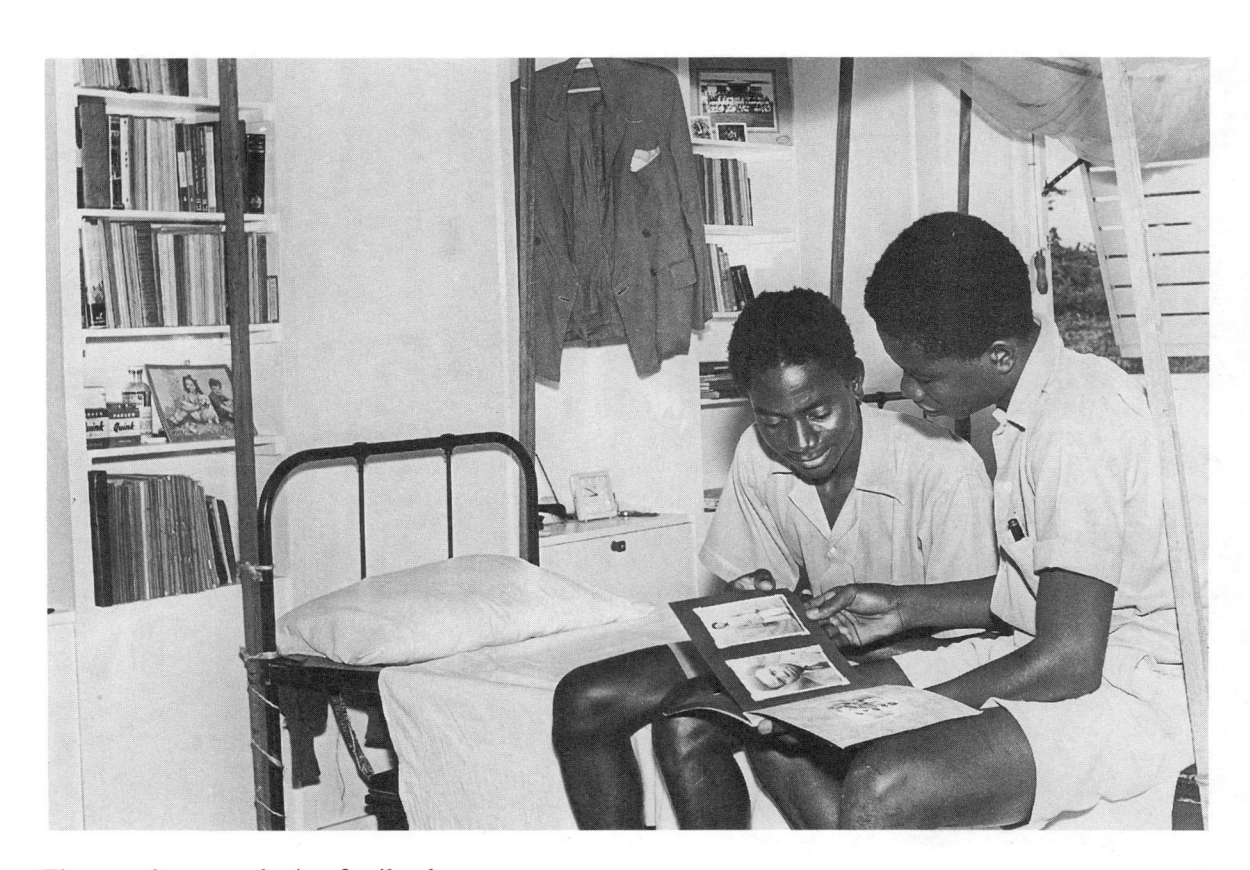

These students are sharing family photos.

Christine X Johnson

SECONDARY GIRLS SCHOOL [52]

Today Ghana has one of the highest educational levels in Africa. She falls within the 20 to 50 percentage world literacy bracket according to United Nations sources.

Ghana spends more on education in relation to her national income than any other country in the world.

Profound changes have been wrought in education in Ghana in the last ten years. Education has served to make the people, especially the children, more respective to new ideas and more aware of what goes on in the world at large. From 1951 educational facilities expanded rapidly and extended to all parts of the country, so that by 1961 they were sufficient to make it possible for the Government to introduce compulsory primary education.

QUESTIONS
1. What does Ghana have today?
2. What does Ghana spend more money on?
3. What profound changes are there in education in Ghana?
4. When did compulsory education begin? Why was it possible?

WORDS

Look up in the dictionary and use in a sentence.

1. Levels
2. Percentage
3. Bracket
4. Sources
5. Nation
6. Profound
7. Wrought
8. Served
9. Expand
10. Sufficient

[52] *Ghana Today*, vol. 1, November 13, 1957.

A Secondary School for girls.

SECONDARY HIGH SCHOOL
ACHOMOTO, GHANA — DR. C. CHAPMAN, PRINCIPAL [53]

Schools since the British left:

1957	Primary Schools	3,372	1963	6,034
	Middle Schools	931		1,252

Enrollment in schools since the British left:

1957	Primary Enrollment	455,749	1963	700,980
	Middle Schools	115,831		160,000
	Secondary High	9,860		23,000
	Technical Institute	2,720		4,000
	Training Colleges	3,873		6,000
	University	785		2,000

Primary and middle schools are entirely free and compulsory. Parents pay no fees and buy no books. Secondary school students are also supplied free books. From this you can see the tremendous advance of education in six or seven years that Ghana has had its independence.

[53] *Ghana Coup*, C. Johnson, pg. 1.

QUESTIONS
1. Give the Primary enrollment 1957-1963.
2. Give the Secondary enrollment 1957-1963.

QUESTIONS continued
3. Give the Technical enrollment 1957-1963.
4. Give the Training College enrollment 1957-1963.
5. Give the Higher Education enrollment 1957-1963.

WORDS

Look up in the dictionary and use in a sentence.

1. Enrollment
2. Primary
3. Secondary
4. Compulsory
5. Tremendous
6. Advances

These students ae among the first to occupy the University College buildings at Legon near Accra, September 1952.

Christine X Johnson

FREE EDUCATION
IN SECONDARY SCHOOLS [54]

The Universal Declaration of Human Rights, adopted unanimously by the General Assembly of the United Nations at its third session on December 10, 1948, states in Article 26; (1) "Everyone has the right to education. Education shall be free at least in the elementary and fundamental stages. Elementary education shall be compulsory."

Ghana takes pride in the fact it has fully subscribed to this declaration. Today the country offers free and compulsory primary education; secondary or higher technical education also became fee-free from September, 1965. University education has always been entirely free in the country, including room, board and tuition.

QUESTIONS
1. Who has the rights of education?
2. Shall education become compulsory?
3. What does the company offer?
4. When did secondary or higher technical become fee-free?

WORDS

Look up in the dictionary and use in a sentence.

1. Universal
2. Declaration
3. Adopted
4. Unanimously
5. Elementary
6. Fundamental
7. Subscribed
8. Compulsory
9. Technical
10. Education

[54] *Ghana*, pg. 8.

Life in Secondary Schools.

COMMONWEALTH HALL
UNIVERSITY COLLEGE [55]

University education has not lagged behind in expansion and development. In 1957 Ghana had two budding universities - The University College at Achimoto and the Kumasi College of Science and Technology. The total enrollment of these two institutions was 785. Now these two institutions have become full fledged universities, called the University of Ghana and the Kwame Nkrumah University of Science and Technology.

A third university, the University College of Cape Coast has been established; and a fourth University College of Agriculture - is being planned. Present enrollment in the three universities is 3,480.

QUESTIONS

1. What were Ghana's 2 universities in 1957?
2. What was the total enrollment?
3. What is the name of the third university?
4. What is the present enrollment of the universities?

WORDS

Look up in the dictionary and use in a sentence.

1. Commonwealth
2. Education
3. Budding
4. Science
5. Institutions
6. Established
7. Agriculture
8. Enrollment
9. Expansion
10. Technology

[55] *Ghana Today*, vol. 1, no. 20, November 27, 1957.

Commonwealth Hall, University College of Ghana.

Christine X Johnson

UNIVERSITY OF GHANA - LEGON [56]

Basic changes are being introduced which will result in considerable saving in time required to complete segments of the educational program. These reductions in the lengthening of the educational cycles will provide increased numbers of school leavers to qualify for employment within the period of the plan. The reductions are being carried out without lowering the educational standards. This has been accomplished by the introduction of modern teaching materials and revisions in the courses of study.

The success of the seven-year plan is finally dependent upon the abilities and the honest hard work of the people who are charged with the responsibility of carrying out the activities required by the plan. About 1,100,000 fresh employees are called for by 1970 to fill all the new jobs which will be created, and to replace those who leave the labor force during the seven year period. Of this total, nearly half must be prepared for employment in the skilled and higher level occupations, ranging from artesians to teachers and other professional occupations. With these heavy demands for trained manpower in mind it is necessary to expand and adjust the educational system accordingly.

[56] *Ghana Today*, vol. 1, no. 17, October 16, 1957.

QUESTIONS

1. How are reductions being carried out?
2. What basic changes are being introduced?
3. How many employees are needed by 1970?
4. What must they be prepared for?

WORDS

Look up in the dictionary and use in a sentence.

1. Basic
2. Introduced
3. Considerable
4. Cycles
5. Increased
6. Lowering
7. Reductions
8. Employment
9. Accomplished
10. Revisions

University of Ghana, Legon.

VOLTA RIVER DAM [57]

The dam at Akosombo was completed ahead of schedule in February 1965, and electrical power began to flow from the power station to various parts of the country in September of the same year. Upon final completion of the project, Ghana's electric capacity will be increased by nearly 500 percent. Half of the power is available for accelerating the diversification of industry and agriculture on which Ghana has embarked, for domestic consumption and for export.

[57] *Facts on Ghana*, pg. 54.

QUESTIONS
1. When was the dam at Akosombo completed?
2. What year?
3. When did electrical power begin to flow?
4. When completed, what will be the electrical capacity?

WORDS
Look up in the dictionary and use in a sentence.

1. Completed
2. Schedule
3. Electrical
4. Various
5. Capacity
6. Available

The Volta River Dam

Christine X Johnson

THE ADOMI BRIDGE
OVER THE VOLTA RIVER [58]

Roads are being cut through the forests. Road building is one of the largest parts of the development plan. New bridges, such as the Adomi bridge bring the country closer together.

The country's trunk road mileage has increased appreciably since the end of World War II, from 2,000 miles, of which only 300 miles were bitumen surfaced, to over 4,000 miles of which over 2,000 miles are bitumen surfaced. In addition over 15,000 miles of drivable roads are maintained by regional organizations and municipal councils.

[58] *Ghana*, pg. 21.

QUESTIONS
1. What does the Adomi bridge do?
2. What was the trunk line mileage before World War II?
3. How are the roads surfaced?

WORDS
Look up in the dictionary and use in a sentence.

1. Forest
2. Bridges
3. Trunk
4. Mileage
5. Maintained
6. Municipal
7. Surface
8. Bitumen

The Adomi Bridge accross the Volta River.

AKOSOMBO DAM [59]

The Volta River project is a vast hydro-electric complex which holds the key to Ghana's industrial development and prosperity. It consists of a high dam at Akosombo, a power house capable of producing 589 M W electrical energy in the initial phase and 883 minimal watts in the final stage, and a transmission system which will deliver electrical energy to the aluminum in the principal towns and villages in southern Ghana.

[59] *Facts on Ghana*

QUESTIONS
1. What is the Volta River project?
2. What does it consist of?
3. What will it deliver?

WORDS
Look up in the dictionary and use in a sentence.

1. Project
2. Volta
3. Hydro-electric
4. Complex
5. Industrial
6. Consist
7. Akosombo
8. Energy
9. Transmission
10. River

Akosombo Dam

Christine X Johnson

POLICE PATROL [60]

The police look through tunnels to find clues to something pertaining to criminals. No guns are ever used, and they do bring the criminals to justice.

Eighteen selected police inspectors are to be trained this year for accelerated promotion to the commissioned ranks of the Ghana Police Force. Vacancies have been obtained for twelve of the inspectors to begin a training course of 18 weeks at Wakefield.

[60] *Ghana Today*, 1957, pg. 9.

QUESTIONS
1. Where do the police look for clues?
2. Do they bring the criminal to justice?
3. How many police inspectors are to be trained?
4. Where will it be held?

WORDS
Look up in the dictionary and use in a sentence.
1. Tunnels   4. Inspectors
2. Clue   5. Promotion
3. Pertaining   6. Justice

Here a patrolman is using a flashlight to search for clues.

BOAKYE - UNITED MATTRESS FACTORY

In Edward Boayke's factory, girls are sewing mattress covers. Eddie went to school at Dunbar Trade School in Chicago, Illinois, U.S.A. for his training. Now he has a large factory in Accra, Ghana.

He says: "By processing materials which are at present exported in their primary state, Ghana will obtain several advantages. First, this will increase the earnings of foreign exchange, since it will be sold at a higher price than those in the raw state. Second, it will increase employment. And third, it will tend to widen the range of our customers, thus spreading the risks of unforeseen or large fluctuations in our sales to individual countries which are the bane of primary producers."

QUESTIONS
1. Where did Edward Boayke go to school?
2. What does he have in Ghana?
3. What advantages will Ghana obtain?

WORDS

Look up in the dictionary and use in a sentence.

1. Factory
2. Sewing
3. Mattresses
4. Processing
5. Material
6. Exported
7. Advantage
8. Foreign
9. Employment

[61] *Ghana Today*, vol. 5 no. 1, March 1, 1961.

This woman is a factory worker using a power machine to make the sides of the mattress.

Christine X Johnson

THE I.D.C. MATCH FACTORY [62]
AT KADE, GHANA

With an authorized capital of $200,000 the match manufacturing firm was set up at Kade, in an area close to the necessary timber supplies.

It has proved a profitable undertaking. Cylinders carry part of the output of the I.D.C. Match Company. It provides work for many of the people in the area.

[62] *Reports and Accounts*, April 1958, pg. 19.

QUESTIONS
1. How much capital did the firm have?
2. What is the area close to?
3. Is it profitable?
4. Who does it provide work for?

WORDS
Look up in the dictionary and use in a sentence.
1. Authorized
2. Firm
3. Necessary
4. Timber
5. Profitable
6. Cylinder

The I.D.C. Match Factory in Kade, Ghana.

SHALLOTS FROM KETA MARKET [63]

Around the Keta Market the people are fat, jovial "Market Mammies." Most women in the Keta are petty traders. The market is always crowded with women who make up about 95% of the traders and customers. Keta Market days which are always regarded as days of merry making are held once in every six days. People come from far and near, on horseback, and in "Mammy Trucks" to sell and buy, returning to their villages late in the evening.

[63] *Ghana: Main Towns and Cities*, pg. 44.

QUESTIONS
1. Who are the traders in Keta?
2. What is the market crowed with?
3. What are the Keta Market days?
4. Where do people come from?

WORDS
Look up in the dictionary and use in a sentence.

1. Jovial   5. Regarded
2. Traders   6. Trucks
3. Customers   7. Return
4. Market   8. Village

Shallots from Keta Market.

Christine X Johnson

BOLGA BASKETS AT KETA MARKET [64]

The salespeople line both sides of the street, and expose for sale every sort of article . . . here are dozens of women offering baskets for sale . . . itinerant peddlers, vendors of gaudy colored handkerchiefs for the head . . . some of the more enterprising have three of the trays before them, with a varied assortment . . . tobacco, dried leaves, pipes . . . coarse knives, small looking glasses and matches.

[64] *Africa Today*, pg. 4.

QUESTIONS
1. What do salespeople do?
2. What do the more enterprising do?
3. Name 6 things that the people sell?

WORDS
Look up in the dictionary and use in a sentence.

1. Expose
2. Articles
3. Offering
4. Itinerant
5. Vendors
6. Enterprising
7. Handkerchief
8. Varied
9. Assortment
10. Coarse

Bolga Baskets lined up for sale.

CROPS SOLD AT MAKOLA MARKET [65]

Along the coast, lagoons, and the Volta River, the chief occupation is fishing, farming and stock raising. In the Keta areas there are large coconut plantations which form the basis of an export industry in Copra. The widespread crop is Cassava and in some places interlock with okra, peppers, tomatoes and eggs. Maize is also grown in large quantities. In the eastern part of the Volta Delta, between Keta and Anlogn, onions are grown on a large commercial scale. Coffee is also grown on a large scale in the Kpandu and Buem-Krache district.

[65] *Africa Today*, pg. 4.

QUESTIONS
1. What is the chief occupation along the coast and other regions?
2. What is in the Keta region?
3. Is maize grown?
4. Where do onions grow?

WORDS
Look up in the dictionary and use in a sentence.

1. Lagoon
2. Occupation
3. Export
4. Industry
5. Maize
6. Commercial
7. Interlock
8. District

Girl with fruit at Marola Market.

Christine X Johnson

THE MAKOLA - ACCRA GHANA [66]

The market does not change much with time. A description written in 1874 still holds in part today, except for the wider variety and more modern kinds of goods obtainable now.

The majority of the sales women were dealers in eatables. Bananas, pineapples, shallots, kanki (Kenke) which is a preparation of ground corn, sold wrapped up in palm leaves in the shape of pasta, groundnuts, eggs, fowl, and cooked meats in various forms.

[66] *Ghana at a Glance*, pg. 38.

QUESTIONS
1. Who deals in eatables?
2. Has the market changed?
3. What is Kenke?

WORDS
Look up in the dictionary and use in a sentence.

1. Written
2. Variety
3. Obtainable
4. Preparation
5. Various
6. Ornaments
7. Wrapped
8. Eatables
9. Palm
10. Fowl

A young girl selling tomatoes at the market.

SALAGA MARKET [67]

At the Salaga Market the vendors sell vegetables, meats, artifacts and other things to the people who attend. If you are a tourist you can get good buys at the market.

In the Northern Savannahs, agriculture is almost entirely confined to the raising of cattle and the cultivation of cereals and other crops e.g., yams, cotton, groundnuts and legumes. There is a notable export of livestock, poultry and yams to the southern regions of the country. Another widespread export of the North is shea butter which is obtained from the fruit of the shea-tree, found growing wild all over the region.

[67] *Ghana at a Glance*, pg. 29.

QUESTIONS
1. What do they sell at the Salaga market?
2. What do they grow in the Northern Savannah?
3. What do they export to the southern region?
4. What is found growing wild all over the region?

WORDS
Look up in the dictionary and use in a sentence.

1. Tourist
2. Savannah
3. Cultivation
4. Cereals
5. Legumes
6. Groundnuts
7. Poultry
8. Shea-tree
9. Export
10. Regions

A view of the Salaga Market.

Christine X Johnson

WEAVING THE KENTE CLOTH [68]

This man is weaving on the traditional loom used in Ghana for many generations. This is how Kente cloth is made and this man is doing the weaving.

With locally grown cotton, a craftsman works with a hand loom of ancient design. He makes strips of cloth about three inches wide, which are stitched side by side into a single garment. The cloth is from the Ashanti region where it is made.

[68] *Ghana Today*, 1962, pg. 8.

QUESTIONS
1. How is Kente cloth made?
2. Where is the cotton grown?
3. In what region is it made?

WORDS
Look up in the dictionary and use in a sentence.

1. Weaving
2. Ancient
3. Design
4. Garment
5. Craftsman
6. Loom
7. Cotton
8. Stitched

Notice how the man weaving the Kente cloth uses both his hands and his feet.

MAKING KENTE CLOTH [69]

In Ghana two men are weaving and sewing Kente cloth. This cloth is worn by the people in the National Assembly. It is to be found only in Ghana.

The hand woven Kente cloth which is fast becoming a national dress is also rich in design and meaning. The Adwensa (meaning) "I have put all ideas into this design," is of a completed design predominately yellow in color. The Abaware (Abaware is the name of a small bird regarded as the Queen Mother of all birds), has a black background with a weft pattern of vertical bands of white, yellow, crimson and green. The oldest industries of Kumasi include the Kente cloth.

QUESTIONS
1. Who is Kente cloth worn by?
2. What is the meaning of Adwensa?
3. What is the meaning of Abaware?

WORDS
Look up in the dictionary and use in a sentence.

1. National
2. Weaving
3. Assembly
4. Design
5. Predominately
6. Weft
7. Vertical
8. Crimson
9. Industries
10. Include

[69] *Ghana Today*, May 9, 1962, pg. 7.

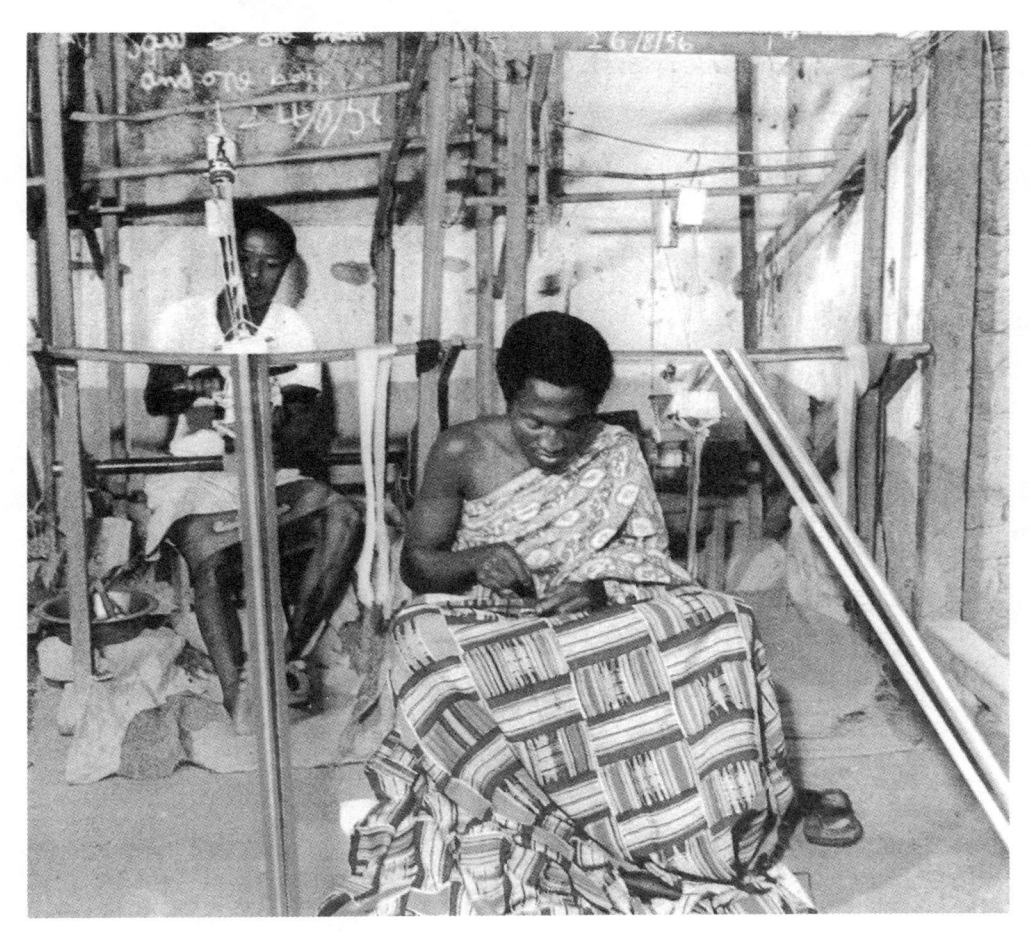

Here the strips of Kente cloth are being sewn together.

Christine X Johnson

AFRICAN DRUMMER [70]

The Africans drummed and danced in the villages at the close of a hard day at work. Music has always played an important part in African life. Each song tells a story, and each dance tells a story. Through their music and art, and dance, they have kept their customs alive, passing them from one generation to another.

Talking drums were made from the skins of female elephants ears. They were used to give notice of danger, a message, fire, death and war. They were the models used to copy our present telegraph system. African drummers could send messages from one part of the country to the other with their "talking drums."

[70] J.D. Shakeford, *The Child's Story of the Negro*, pg. 70.

QUESTIONS
1. What did the Africans do after a long hot day?
2. What has music always done in African life?
3. What has each dance and song tell?
4. What were talking drums made from?
5. What was used as the model for our telegraph system?

WORDS

Look up in the dictionary and use in a sentence.

1. Drummed
2. Danced
3. Village
4. Danger
5. Generation
6. Elephant
7. Message
8. Present
9. Telegraph
10. Models
11. System
12. Country

Talking drums.

DANCING IN GHANA [71]

In traditional dancing all over the country, beauty in the human figure is thought of and expressed in terms of certain definite symbols, every part of the body being expressed in terms of either a circle or an oval.

Ghanaians have several festivals which are celebrated at various times of the year. Though each festival has it's own significance, they are all invariably colorful and often accompanied by every conceivable pomp and gaiety.

Handed down through the ages, the culture of the people is a vital part of their lives.

[71] *Facts on Ghana*, pg. 70.

QUESTIONS

1. How is beauty in the human figure expressed?
2. How are Ghanaian festivals celebrated?
3. What are they accompanied by?

WORDS

Look up in the dictionary and use in a sentence.

1. Traditional
2. Expressed
3. Definite
4. Symbols
5. Pomp
6. Oval
7. Festivals
8. Significance
9. Invariable
10. Conceivable

A group of women enjoying the art of dance.

Christine X Johnson

THE MARIMBA [72]

Long before pianos were made, Africans used an instrument called a "Marimba." The keys were made of palm wood instead of ivory and the players beat upon them with wooden hammers instead of playing on them with their fingers. The musical instrument that Lionel Hampton made famous, called the xylophone looks very much like the Marimba.

Africans were the first people to use stringed instruments long before the European world existed.

[72] Ghana Information, Section Prints, Embassy of Ghana.

QUESTIONS
1. What did the Africans use before pianos were made?
2. What are marimbas made of?
3. Who used the first stringed instrument?

QUESTIONS continued
4. What did the players use instead of fingers?
5. What is the instrument called that looks like a marimba?
6. Who made it famous?

WORDS
Look up in the dictionary and use in a sentence.

1. Pianos
2. Before
3. African
4. Instrument
5. Marimba
6. Existed
7. Palm
8. Instead
9. Players
10. Hammers
11. Fingers
12. Ivory
13. Musical
14. Famous
15. Xylophone

Men playing the Marimba.

DANCING TO XYLOPHONE MUSIC [73]

In traditional dancing all over the country beauty in the human figure is thought of and expressed in terms of certain definite symbols, every part of the body being expressed in terms of either a circle or an oval.

The xylophone is popular all over Africa as a percussive melodic instrument. Some have pet resonators while others use gourds. In an ensemble, two players may play in parallel octaves against counter-rhythms from the other players.

[73] *African Dances*, Okopu & Bell, Institute of African Studies, University of Ghana-Legon, pg. 20.

QUESTIONS
1. What is thought of in symbols?
2. How is the body thought of?
3. Is the xylophone popular?

WORDS
Look up in the dictionary and use in a sentence.
1. Traditional
2. Percussion
3. Expressed
4. Symbols
5. Definite
6. Xylophone
7. Gourds
8. Octaves
9. Parallel
10. Ensemble

A group of girls dancing to Xylophone music.

Christine X Johnson

GHANA AIRWAYS [74]

Ghana has since, the attainment of Independence in 1957, embarked upon a big program of expansion in all spheres of her air service, to bring them in line with her status as an African State of international importance.

In keeping with the spirit of African Independence, freedom and unity, Ghana Airways - the National Airline - has been flying high the flag of Ghana into various parts of the world.

Many of the independent African states have now been linked by air. A route recently inaugurated is a link from Accra and Beruit via Cairo.

Originally run in conjunction with British Overseas Airways Corporation, Ghana Airways was established in July, 1958 and started operation in October of that year. Since then, its growth has been phenomenal. To give it a truly Ghanaian character and to help project the "African Personality," the Ghana Government has bought the shareholding of the BOAC Associated Company LTD., that formally operated the airline, thereby giving it an independent status as well.

Ghana Airways, now owns and operates a fleet of 17 aircraft. The Ghana Airways reorganization programme has necessitated a change in color under which the airline flies. The new color consists in the main, of light blue and white with a Kente cloth motif. The Ghana flag is painted to cover the whole of the rudder.

To enlarge and reequip the present fleet, contracts have been placed for the Ghana Airways with an even greater confidence, and determination to help implement the governments' declared policy of carrying the Ghana and the African personality to all parts of the continent, and eventually to all corners of the world.

[74] *Ghana Builds*, Republican Embassy Issue, vol. 1, no.2, July 1961.

QUESTIONS
1. What has Ghana embarked upon since independence?
2. When did Ghana Airways start operation?
3. What did the Ghana government do to help project the African personality?
4. How many aircraft does Ghana own?
5. What is the motif on the Ghana aircraft?

WORDS
Look up in the dictionary and use in a sentence.

1. Aircraft
2. Attainment
3. Embarked
4. Status
5. Spheres
6. National
7. Various
8. Route
9. Inaugurated
10. Originally

Preparing for departure.

GHANA'S OWN SHIPPING LINE [75]

On September 10, 1957, Ghana decided to inaugurate her own shipping line. For decades, even centuries, ships from foreign ports have come to Ghana with goods from abroad and have left with raw materials for countries all over the world; but none of these ever flew the colors that were Ghana's own. It was understandable, for Ghana was still a colonial territory and was therefore not responsible for her own destiny. It was not surprising that barely six months after the attainment of independence Ghana decided to have her own shipping line.

The Black Star line started with only one ship, the Volta River. The President, himself, was at Takoradi to greet the officers and crew of the ship on its maiden voyage along the southern coast of Ghana.

Working on the ships of the line are hundreds of Ghanaian young men, who after courses of study are putting their knowledge to practice on the ships. Many of them have acquired responsible positions on the ships and the day is not far when all officers and ratings will be Ghanaian.

From the ports of Tema, Takoradi and Accra, the Black Star line sails to ports all over the world flying the colors of the Republic of Ghana.

There are not Ghanaians more proud than the officers and men who man the ships of the Black Star line. For these young men a new vista has opened and the lust for travel to other lands to meet and see other people has become more irresistible. The romance of the strange lands and the call of the sea have found many willing and enthusiastic "victims" among the young men of Ghana.

The more remarkable achievement of the very new shipping line is that since its inauguration on September 10, 1957, it has incurred no losses. That is an achievement to be proud of.

The day is not far when at any time a ship of the Black Star line can be found berthed in all the important ports of the world flying the flag of the Freedom of Africa.

[75] *Ghana Builds*, Republican Embassy Issue, vol. 1, no.2, July 1961.

QUESTIONS

1. When did Ghana inaugurate her own shipping line?
2. How long have ships from abroad come to our land?
3. How long after independence did Ghana decide to own her own shipping line?
4. How many ships did the Black Star line start with?
5. What colors do the ships fly?

WORDS

Look up in the dictionary and use in a sentence.

1. Decides
2. Shipping
3. Centuries
4. Decades
5. Foreign
6. Colors
7. Territory
8. Crew
9. Acquired
10. Vista

Black Star shipping line.

Christine X Johnson

GEORGE - AT THE NURSING SCHOOL [76]

George and his mother live in New York City. They came to Ghana to learn more about the country.

It is the determination to ensure the highest standards of health for the people by providing parallel services in both curative and preventative medicine. In carrying out both these responsibilities emphasis is on preventative medicine which will continue to have a clearly defined priority. The training of doctors and nurses, and midwives to man hospital services in the country is being pursued. At present 1,385 nurses are being trained in various institutions under the ministry. They are doing the best post-basic nursing educational course at the University of Ghana.

QUESTIONS
1. What has a clearly defined priority?
2. What kind of training is being pursued?
3. How many nurses are trained?
4. Where is it being carried out?

WORDS

Look up in the dictionary and use in a sentence.

1. Determination
2. Providing
3. Parallel
4. Curative
5. Preventative
6. Responsibility
7. Emphasis
8. Defined
9. Priority
10. Institutions

[76] *Ghana Today*, 1965, pg. 4.

George visiting the nursing school.

MARIE LOUISE CHILDREN'S HOSPITAL[77]

George visited Marie Louise Children's Hospital in Accra and helped distribute vitamins.

As well as being concerned with a long term program of maternal and child welfare services in the framework of the Government's Second Development Plan, the scheme will strengthen the basis for the sound training of Rural Health Workers and "will also lead to the expansion of the network of health centers throughout the Country."

[77] *Ghana Today*, October 2, 1957, vol 16, pg. 6.

QUESTIONS
1. What was George doing at the hospital?
2. What will the scheme strengthen?

WORDS
Look up in the dictionary and use in a sentence.

1. Distribute
2. Vitamins
3. Concerned
4. Program
5. Material
6. Welfare
7. Scheme
8. Services
9. Network
10. Country

These children live in an orphanage attached to a hospital in the Eastern Region.

Christine X Johnson

KUMASI GENERAL HOSPITAL [78]
and the NURSES TRAINING SCHOOL, Kumasi Ashanti, Ghana

One of the finest medical institutions in the whole of Africa can be found in Kumasi. Containing many specialist departments the Kumasi General Hospital cost about 2,500,000 to build. The hospital is equipped with the most up-to-date medical equipment and is the largest in Ghana. Other new hospitals have recently been opened in various parts of the country, some were built by Missions, and many existing hospitals, particularly the main hospital in Accra at Korle Bu, are being extended and improved.

Since the early fifties the health services in Ghana have undergone an extensive transformation, especially the new 500 bed hospital at Kumasi, highlight the physical expansion.

The first choice of a career for many educated girls is nursing. The nurses training scheme received a major impetus in 1945 with the opening of the first Nurse's Training College at Accra. The nurse training facilities at the new Kumasi Hospital are probably unsurpassed in Africa.

On the grounds of the Kumasi General Hospital is the legendary sword of Okombo Anopye, who is said to have invoked from the sky the Golden Stool which binds the Ashanti people together. This sword was planted in the ground by the great priest as a symbol of the unification of the Ashanti people. It has never been withdrawn and it is believed that the day the sword comes out of the ground will mark the end of the Ashanti Nation.

[78] *Ghana Today*, May 9, 1962, vol. 6, no. 5, pg. 7.

QUESTIONS
1. Where can you find the largest and finest medical institution in Ghana?
2. What is found on the grounds of the hospital?
3. What will mark the end of the Ashanti Nation?
4. What is the first choice of a career for educated Ashanti girls?

WORDS
Look up in the dictionary and use in a sentence.

1. Department
2. Hospital
3. Legendary
4. Golden
5. Together
6. Unification
7. Grand
8. Mark
9. Undergone
10. Transformation
11. Equipped
12. Medical
13. Recently
14. Scheme
15. Extended
16. Impetus

General Hospital and Nurses' Training school.

KUMASI FORT [79]

In the Kumasi Fort, the British were starved out. They ate their saddles, rats and anything they could find until help came. The people of Ghana fought the British hard and held out for 30 years, until they were defeated.

The Kumasi Fort is one of the main attraction landmarks in Kumasi. It was built in 1816 with stones from the Palace of the Asantehene, Nana Osei Tutu Kwame. It is now a military museum. One of the finest medical institutions in the whole of Africa can be found in Kumasi.

[79] *Ghana Main Towns and Cities*, pg. 34.

QUESTIONS
1. How long did Kumasi fight the British?
2. What did the British eat to stay alive?
3. When was the Kumasi Fort built?
4. What is the Kumasi Fort used for today?

WORDS
Look up in the dictionary and use in a sentence.

1. Starved
2. Defeated
3. Palace
4. Landmark
5. Museum
6. Military

Kumasi Fort.

Christine X Johnson

AMY A. GARVEY

In 1957 I met Amy A. Garvey at Dr. Danquah's house for dinner. She told me that after her husband, Marcus Garvey was taken to England and put in jail, they were divorced and she migrated to Africa.

She sent her car for me and a young man from New York to come to Kumasi. We went and stayed in her home.

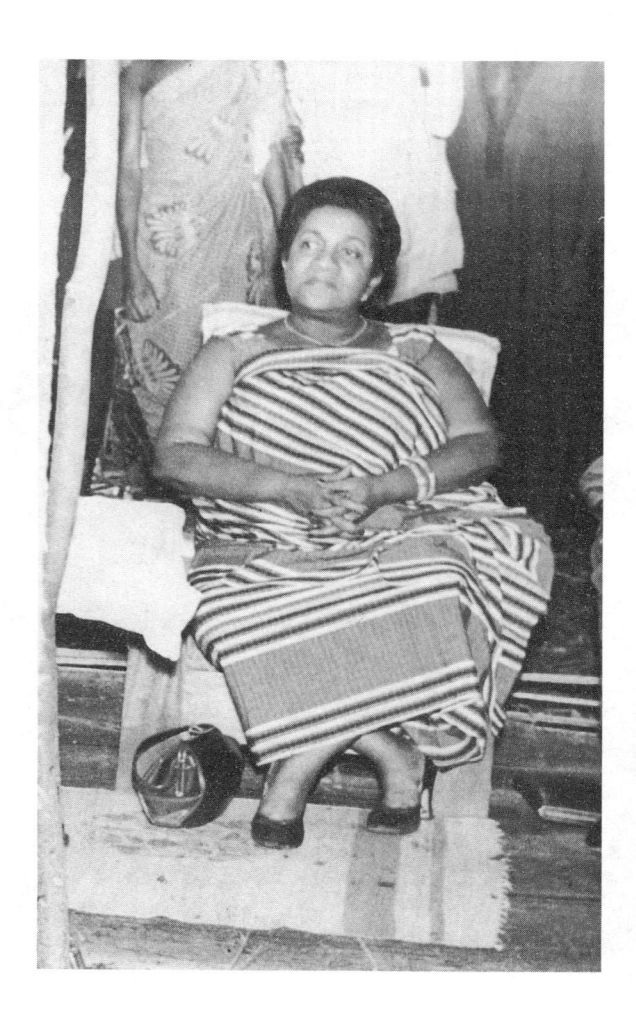

After coming there she took us to see the "Asantehene" and later to the dedication of her school. She played a great part in the restructure of Kumasi. Later she returned to the United States in New York, where she lived quietly and later died.

QUESTIONS
1. What happened to Mrs Garvey's husband?
2. When did I meet Mrs. Garvey?
3. What did we do while visiting Mrs. Garvey in Kumasi?
4. What happened when she returned to New York?

WORDS

Look up in the dictionary and use in a sentence.

1. Jail
2. Migrated
3. Dedication
4. School
5. Restructure
6. Return
7. Quietly
8. Played

Amy A. Garvey, wife of Marcus Garvey.

Mrs. Garvey's home.

Photos by Christine Johnson

Ghana Under Nkrumah

ASANTEHENE AND THE GOLDEN STOOL [80]

The golden stool is regarded as the symbol of Asantehene's authority and as the cultural and political unity of the people. This stool is believed to have been invoked from the Heavans by Okomfo Anokye on a Friday, hence its name "Asikadwa Kofi" (Golden Stool Kofi).

It was on this occasion that the chief Priest announced the rites by which the stool was to be regularly "fed and purified." The foundation of Adac festival with its institutional religion also dates from this time.

[80] *Ghana Main Town and Cities*, pg. 32.

QUESTIONS

1. What is the Golden Stool regarded as?
2. Where was it invoked from?
3. What is it's name?
4. What was the regular rites of the stool?

WORDS

Look up in the dictionary and use in a sentence.

1. Regarded
2. Symbol
3. Authority
4. Cultural
5. Political
6. Invoked
7. Occasion
8. Announced
9. Regularly
10. Purified

Asantehene sitting in state with the Golden Stool beside him.

Christine X Johnson

THE SOUL OF ASHANTI [81]

Not mace and orb, but a Golden Stool was the Asantehene's symbol of authority. This stool was the shrine and symbol of the National "Soul of Ashanti." It was always carried in processions covered with a camel's hair umbrella, *The Katamanso*, the "covering of the Nation." The stool, as well as the Asantehene, had attendants, who supported the golden bells which hung from its sides. Gold death masks of great enemies slain by Ashanti were attached to it.

[81] *Ghana Around the World*, pg. 8.

QUESTIONS
1. What was the Ashanti's symbol of authority?
2. What was the National Soul of Ashanti?
3. What is the Katamanso?
4. What was attached to it?

WORDS
Look up in the dictionary and use in a sentence.
1. Mace
2. Golden
3. Authority
4. National
5. Processions
6. Camel
7. Umbrella
8. Attendants
9. Supported
10. Enemies

Chief and retinue, Ghana.

TAMALE, GHANA [82]

Tamale occupies a strategic and central position on the great Northern road stretching from Kumasi to Bolgatanga. With a population of some 60,000 people. Tamale is the administrative capital of the Northern region.

Almost all ceremonies in Tamale are marked by tribal drumming and dancing for which special groups, including the "Bamaya", "Takai" and the "Gooji" troups exist.

Tourist attractions in Tamale include the evergreen Tamale Horticultural Garden, the Gulkpe Na's Palace and tomb of Na-Gbewa, founder of many tribes in North-Eastern Dagomba.

Tamale has been an army center for over 50 years and today two battalions of the Ghana Army are based there.

[82] *Ghana Main Towns and Cities*, pg. 44.

QUESTIONS

1. What does Tamale occupy?
2. What is it's population?
3. What are the ceremonies marked by?
4. What are the tourist atttractions?
5. What has Tamale been?

WORDS

Look up in the dictionary and use in a sentence.

1. Occupies
2. Strategic
3. Stretching
4. Ceremonies
5. Including
6. Tourist
7. Include
8. Horticultural
9. Battalions
10. Tribes

A Northerner in tribal costume.

Christine X Johnson

Nana Osae Djon, Chief of Oburi, Ghana.

GHANA CHIEFS [83]

Nana Ofori Atta II, Chief of the Kibi, an African Chief of remarkable character, who had been one of the African members of the Legislative Council reconstituted in 1916. Under his leadership the African members of the Legislative Council developed steadily in skill and influence. He was the first appointed to the executive council in 1942.

Meanwhile, in 1935, the Ashanti Council, composed of Otumfuo Sir Osei Argyeman Prempeh II and the other representivies of the principal divisions of Ashanti, had been set up as the Supreme Native Authorities for that region.

Ashanti has a rich cultural background and ancient history. The Asantehene and his predecessors have for long ruled the Ashanti people who have been bound together by the Golden Stool. The Golden Stool is regarded as the Soul of Ashanti. It is believed to have come down from heaven in answer to the prayers of the great fetish priest Ofomfo Anokye who lived in Kumasi during the reign of King Osei Tutu, the founder of the Ashanti Dynasty.

[83] *Ghana Main Towns and Cities*, pg. 32; *A Brief Guide to Ghana*, pg. 36; *The Making of Ghana*, pg. 9.

Kumasi, the Capital of Ashanti, is generally called the "Garden City" because of its beautiful lawns and avenues.

Nana Osae Djon one of the Chiefs, was selected because on account of his wide knowledge and experience of local affairs and with a view to representing all sections of the community. This picture (page 94) was sent to me on the visit of the Queen of England to Aburi on November 16, 1961.

QUESTIONS
1. Who was Prempeh II?
2. Who bound the Ashanti people together?
3. What is Kumasi called?
4. What happened under Nana Ofori Atta II?
5. Why was Nana Osa Djon selected?

WORDS
Look up in the dictionary and use in a sentence.

1. Remarkable   6. Principal
2. Members   7. Supreme
3. Council   8. Selected
4. Influence   9. Experience
5. Composed   10. Sections

Sir Osei Agyeman Prempeh II, Asantehene.

Nana Ofori Atta II, Chief of Kibi, Ghana.

Christine X Johnson

GHANA PLAYING HOST
TO FOREIGN DIGNITARIES REPRESENTING EAST AND WEST [84]

Ghana's establishment of Diplomatic missions in Eastern and Western countries is another pointer to her policy of non-alignment and friendly relations with all nations.

A practical step to ease world tension was convening the conference *World Without the Bomb* held in Accra, June 1962, where Madam Tomi Kora, Vice Mayor of Hiroshema, Mangura Kenagua Japan, and Mr. Shinzo, Mayor of Hiroshima were participants. Over 150 experts and observers discussed and considered objectively a number of problems including the reduction of world tension, and the methods of effective inspection and control of disarmament.

[84] *Ghana at a Glance*, pg. 64.

QUESTIONS
1. Who did Ghana play host to?
2. What was the practical step to ease World tension?
3. When was the World Without the Bomb Conference held?
4. Who was Tomi Kora?
5. How many participated in the Conference?

WORDS
Look up in the dictionary and use in a sentence.

1. Host	6. Relations
2. Foreign	7. Nations
3. Dignitaries	8. Experts
4. Missions	9. Objectively
5. Policy	10. Tensions

Madam Tomi Kora, Vice Mayor of Hiroshema, and Mr. Shinzo, Mayor of Hiroshima.

WOMEN OF AFRICA
AND OF AFRICAN DESCENT [85]

President Nkrumah said: "Today, African people and people of African descent all over the world are seeking a new way out of the conditions which seperated us for so long, in this they are taking their lives in their own hands. Hold on forever, with much of Black emancipation. The long Black struggle is not only against imperialism, neo-colonialism and racism, but also the deep mystic colonialism, the kind you are frequently experiencing within the United States of America.

In the final analysis our survival tactics depend upon our combined strength and energies and our sufferings unto us. This is the time that Black America should join hands with their Brothers and Sisters in the great task heralding Black honor and dignity. This conference of African Women and Women of African Descent representing various womens organizations in Africa in 1962, to Shirley Graham DuBois and women from the United States, I wish you well, I salute you. Mother Africa salutes you."

[85] *Ghana at a Glance*, pgs. 62-63.

QUESTIONS
1. When was the first Womens Conference held?
2. Who took part in the conference?
3. Who is taking their lives in their own hands?
4. What was Ghana's aim?

WORDS
Look up in the dictionary and use in a sentence.

1. Organized
2. Economic
3. Include
4. Descent
5. Various
6. Policy
7. Participated
8. Representing
9. Objective
10. Instrumental

Dr. Kwame Nkrumah speaking to the conference. Seated center is author, far right is Shirley DuBois.

Christine X Johnson

WILLIAM E.B. DuBOIS
WORLD WITHOUT THE BOMB CONFERENCE [86]

Osaygefo said: "In the face of the catastrophe that menaces the world; any person, body, or government which refuses the olive branch of 'Live and let live' extended to all by the Accra Assembly cannot but be insane and should be denounced. War-mongering is anti-socialist and a crime." W.E.B. DuBois and Dr. Johnson looked on and smiled. This was the last conference Dr. W.E.B. DuBois and Dr. Johnson came to.

Dr. DuBois later said: "One thing alone I charge you, as you live, believe in life; always human beings will live and progress to greater broader and fuller lives."

This was the good-bye to the world he had struggled in so long. He was to writing the history of the Black man in the world what Picasso is to the white world of art. He and Shirley Graham DuBois, his wife are interred in a shrine at the DuBois Research Center in Accra.

[86] *The Ghanian*, August 8, 1962, pgs. 4-9.

QUESTIONS
1. What is an anti-socialist crime?
2. Who attended the conference?
3. What did DuBois say?
4. Where is he buried and with whom?

WORDS
Look up in the dictionary and use in a sentence.

1. Catastrophe   5. Extend
2. Menace   6. Denounce
3. Government   7. Crime
4. Refuse   8. Human

Dr. DuBois (center), and Dr. Johnson at the World Without the Bomb conference.

WORLD WITHOUT THE BOMB
WORLD PEACE [87]

Undaunted, Osagyfeo Dr. Kwame Nkrumah, President of Ghana, has done it again. Like the insubmerisble cork, he rides the rough waters of vain criticisms of the unimaginative. Thus he landed home safely the Accra Assembly which convened August 8, 1962.

If the Nuclear Powers turn a deaf ear to reason, it would not be the fault of Osaygefo. He has done his part to save mankind from the grim holocaust of war. With remarkable statesmanship and as a leading citizen of the world, he has led the path to peace.

[87] *The Ghanaian*, August 8, 1962, pgs. 4-9.

QUESTIONS

1. What did Osaygefo do to save mankind?
2. What was he a lifelong citizen of?
3. What would not be the fault of Osaygefo?

WORDS

Look up in the dictionary and use in a sentence.

1. Undaunted
2. President
3. Cork
4. Rough
5. Vain
6. Criticism
7. Landed
8. Nuclear
9. Powers
10. Deaf

Osagyfeo Dr. Kwame Nkrumah addressing the conference.

Christine X Johnson

OSAYGEFO KWAME NKURMAH [88]
PRESIDENT OF GHANA

Upon his death on April 27, 1972 Ghana President Nkrumah's body lay in Conakry, Guinea, the country which granted him sanctuary following his ouster in 1966. His family and Ghanaian officials later reported agreement on the return of his body to his beloved homeland.

At the site of his birthplace, in Nkroful, a grave was dug and lined with marble. A small concrete amphitheater was erected so the leaders of the National Redempton Council - a liberal military regime and others could take part in the interment rites. Kwame Nkrumah's body was re-interred at Accra to a beautiful mausoleum which was constructed on the site of the former polo grounds. The striking marble structure is a fitting memorial to Ghana's first president, the man who led the country to independence.

President Nkrumah made Ghana what it is today, a free and independent African state.

[88] *Chicago Defender*, July 18, 1972, pg. 13.

QUESTIONS
1. Where did Nkrumah die?
2. When did he die?
3. What happened at his birthplace?
4. What has been erected?
5. What did Nkrumah make of Ghana?

WORDS
Look up in the dictionary and use in a sentence.

1. Lay	6. Agreement
2. Sanctuary	7. Body
3. Ouster	8. Site
4. Died	9. Redemption
5. Reported	10. Liberal

The First President of Ghana, His Excellency the Right Honourable Kwame Nkrumah, P.C., M.A., M.Sc., LL.D., was elected on April 27, 1960.

THE WHITE ANT HILL [89]

Out on the African savannahs live a Nomadic tribe of herdsmen whose unique way of life has existed, virtually unchanged for a thousand years.

In the world of the Ewe, a world where home is a mud hut and family encompasses an entire tribe; a world where wild animals roam free and cattle means life; a world rich in superstition, lore and tradition; where the termites sometimes called white ants make tall, hard castles; the Queen of the termites does no work, they have Drones to do all the labor. The Queen lays eggs and the Drones carry them away and put them in storage to hatch. Sometimes the Castle is broken down and the Queen is eaten.

[89] *Growing up Masi*, by Tom Schachtman, photo by Tom Renn.

QUESTIONS
1. Who lives on the savannah? How long have they lived there?
2. What does the Ewe world encompasse?
3. What do cattle mean to the Ewe?
4. What does the Queen termite do?
5. What do the Drones do?

WORDS
Look up in the dictionary and use in a sentence.

1. Savannah
2. Nomad
3. Virtually
4. Unique
5. Existed
6. Encompass
7. Animals
8. Superstition
9. Tradition
10. Supressing

Young people resting at the base of an ant hill.

Christine X Johnson

KWAME NKRUMAH in CHICAGO, ILLINOIS USA

The Honorable Kwame Nkrumah is greeted at the airport by Mayor Daley. July 1958

Congregation of Chicago business men headed by Claude Barnett waiting to greet Kwame Nkrumah at the airport.

School children in Washington Park, celebrating Kwame Nkrumah's visit to Chicago in July, 1958.

The African-American Heritage Association (AAHA) took pictures of Kwame Nkrumah during his visit to Chicago. The photo album was presented to him as a gift. Holding the book is Christine Johnson, president of AAHA. She is joined by Ishmal Flory, director of AAHA and Lula Saffold, a member.

A banquet was held at the Blackstone Hotel in honor of Kwame Nkrumah. Guests at the speakers table include: Etta Moten, Mayor Daley, Kwame Nkrumah and Mrs. Daley, among others.

Other guests at the banquet included Balm Lavell and John Johnson.

Ghana Under Nkrumah

The Honorable Kwame Nkrumah, Premier of Ghana, standing with Christine Johnson, Leo Sparks and Cathern Davis Flory. Chicago, Illinois USA, July 30, 1958.

Christine X Johnson

Ghana Under Nkrumah a Chronology [90]

1909	Born, the village of Nkroful in Nzima. His mother was NYANIBAH. His father, a goldsmith had several wives. He had older brothers and sisters.
1914	He went to school in a one room school house, run by Catholic Missionaries.
1926	Kwame began to teach as a Pupil Teacher when he was 17 years old.
1927	He is invited to come to Accra to the Government Training College.
	Kwame received word that his father had died as a result of an infected foot. His journey took several days, when he arrived home his father had been buried.
1928	Attends the Prince of Wales College.
	Has meeting with Rev. Kegyir Aggrey. Later he was shocked at his death.
1930	Nkrumah accepts a post teaching elementary school in Elmina, and founded the Teachers Association there.
1931	He was appointed Head Teacher at a Catholic School at Axim.
1933	Taught at a Training School for Catholics Priests at Amissano, near Elmina.
	Attends a Teachers Conference in Accra and met Dr. Nandi Azikiwe.
	Resigned his job and made plans to go to Lagos, Nigeria.
	Stowed away on a steamer to Lagos. Got dirty and when he got off the boat he went to the nearest market and bought clothes. Later he went to see his Kinsmen, was warmly welcomed and was given $400. With this money and an additional sum from another relative the Chief of the State of Nsaeum, he had enough to get to America.
	Sitting on his bunk aboard the Apapa before it sailed, he was delivered a telegram from Dr. Azikiwe saying "Good-bye, remember to trust in God and in yourself."
1935	He sailed from Liverpool to New York in the fall.
	He was late in entering Lincoln University where he majored in Economics and Sociology.
	He came back to New York for a summer job in a soap factory but had to give it up because a Doctor said it was affecting his health.
	He got a job as a seaman, washing pots and pans on a ship that sailed from Philadelphia to Mexico.

---

90. *Ghana: The Autobiography of Kwame Nkrumah.* London: Thomas Nelson & Sons, ltd., 1957.

1939 — He graduated from Lincoln University and was offered a job as Assistant Lecturer in Philosophy, first year Greek, and a course in Negro History.

1942 — He led his class at graduation from the Theological Seminary, receiving a Bachelor of Theology degree; received a Masters of Science degree in Education from the University of Pennsylvania.

1943 — Received Masters of Art in Philosophy from the University of Pennsylvania.
He worked with the African Student Association. Founded and edited a paper called the *African Interpreter*.

1945 — In May he left the United States. Attends the 5th Pan African Congress in London. Nkrumah is author of one of the two declarations addressed to the imperialist powers of the world adopted by the Congress, Dr. DuBois wrote the other.

He was absorbed in England with West African friends like Jomo Kenyetta, Wallace Johnson, Kojo Botsio and others.

1946 — *Towards Colonial Freedom* published.

1947 — He received an invitation from Dr. J.B. Danquah, leader of a newly formed organization, the United Gold Coast Convention, to return to his country and serve as general secretary. As he waited to board the steamer at Liverpool in November, he approached by the police, who took his passport and questioned him at length, finally they handed him back his passport and allowed him to embark.

He went to Tarkwa where he found Ackah Watson, and met his mother so they could be quietly alone. When they finally met he was shocked at the change in his mother after twelve years, and she in him.

Finally he spoke at Tarkwa, a mining town, to a schoolhouse full of people. He traced the history of relations between the English and the Gold Coast. He made a passionate plea for action and ended by saying "If in the past you have been sleeping, wake up now!" Then an elderly man arose pointing to Nkrumah saying "This young man is God's greatest gift to the Gold Coast. Hear you him." Applause broke out all over the hall.

1948 — January 1st, Nkrumah went to Saltpond to begin his work as Secretary of the United Gold Coast Convention. It was clear that there was not enough money to pay him $400.00 as promised, this was to lure him from London. He told the shocked Convention that he did not want any money at all. If they would take care of his room and board and provide him with some kind of car. They looked at him in amazement. These men had incomes of about $10 -12 thousand dollars a year. They thought him queer as their Secretary but they admired his energy and enthusiasm and finally worked out on an assignment for a salary of $100.00 per month and a car.

Nkrumah immediately set up an office in Saltpond with one typist as his "staff." He traveled all over the country. At his rallies the people flocked to him. He always sat down with the simple people and ate the simplest of meals.

Finally riots broke out in Accra, many people were killed. They were looking for Nkrumah when a woman took him in her house. He felt like he was getting her into trouble, so he sneaked out and returned to Saltpond unobserved. There he found his office padlocked by the police. He moved to Cape Coast and had been there a few days when the police broke into his room and arrested him. He was put into a van with other members of the UGCC, Dr. Danquah, Ako Ako Adjei, W. Ofori Atta, Akufo Addo and E.O. Lamptey. They were all put on a plane and taken to a prison in Kumasi, the capital of Ashanti.

In Lawra he was suddenly released. He founded the *Accra Evening News* with Komla Gbedemah serving as editor, the 1st edition was printed September 3rd.

1949 On June 12th 60,000 men and women gave Nkrumah a deafening welcome when Nkrumah announced the formation of the Convention People's Party (C.P.P.), and the main slogan would be "Self Government Now!" He also explains the C.P.P.s campaign of Positive Action, leading to strikes and disorder. Nkrumah and others were jailed for sedition.

In jail he wrote on toilet paper to the outside world.

1950 A landslide victory for the C.P.P.

On February 13th, Nkrumah got out of jail. He meets Sir Charles Arden-Clarke at Christinaborg.

1951 In June he receives a Doctor of Laws degree from Lincoln University. He nominates his Cabinet and begins to fulfill his campaign promises.

1954 Kwame Nkrumah becomes Prime Minister.
Photo page xvii: The Prime Minister, Hon Kwame Nkrumah, LLD, MP (centre, seated), and his cabinet. Standing, left to right: Hon A Ofori Atta, MP; Hon N.A. Welbeck, MP; Hon B. Yeboah Afari, MP; Hon F.H. Allassani, MP; Hon J.B. Erzuah, MP; Hon L.R. Abavana, MP; Hon Ako Adjei, MP; Hon Krobo Edusei, MP. Seated, left to right: Hon A.E. Inkumsah, MP; Hon Kojo Botsio, MP; Hon Kwame Nkrumah, LLD, MP; Hon K.A. Gbedemah, MP; Hon A. Casely Hayford, MP.

He makes tours of the country to represent the people. A bomb is placed under his home, which damaged his mothers apartment. She is not hurt.

1956 Victory for Nkrumah and Governor Arden-Clarke, when a note from the Secretary of State stated: "Her Majesty would at the first opportunity introduce a bill into the United Kingdom Parliament to accord independence to the Gold Coast, and that subjected to Parliament approval Her Majesty's government intended that full independence should come about March 6, 1957."

1957 *Ghana: The Autobiography of Kwame Nkrumah* published.

The Duchess of Kent and about 22 delegates from foreign nations arrived.

Mrs. Louis Armstrong (wife of famed musician), teaches Nkrumah to dance with the Duchess. The Duchess reads a message from the Queen saying: "My government in the Untied Kingdom has ceased from this day to have any authority in Ghana."

The large star in the Ghanian flag that was raised at one minute after midnight on March 6, 1957, stressed the idea that Ghana was a "lodestar" on the First day of Independence.

Nkrumah marries Ms. Fathia Halen Ritzk of Egypt in December.

Volta River is dependent on Second Development Plan. A large aluminum smelter is part of the scheme.

1960   Kwame Nkrumah is elected President April 27th, and Ghana becomes a Republic on July 1st.

1961   *I Speak of Freedom* is published.
A large statue of Kwame Nkrumah is erected in front of the Parliament Building in Accra, on its base reads Kwame Nkrumah, Founder of the nation of Ghana. It was destroyed in 1966 when he was disposed. The current leader of Ghana, Rawlings, has since restored it.

University College near Accra is a source of pride to the President.

Many students go to foreign countries to study. Many students join the builders brigade to work on collective farms.

He has a bungalow on the beach near Half Assini to retreat when he needs solitude.

1966   When he was disposed Sekou Toure said "My home is your home." Nkrumah was given a great welcome in Guinea.

On April 12th he wrote to his American friends care of the author of *Ghana Under Nkrumah*; reliving his student days in the United States and reflecting on the years of service to his people, he wrote:

Mrs. Christine C. Johnson, President
African-American Heritage Association
306 East 43rd Street
Chicago, Illinois USA

    I don't think you should worry about me. What has happened has given me time to take stock of my work for Ghana and Africa during the past 20 years. New vistas, new perspectives, new avenues seem to open up more clearly. Do not be mad and disgusted with Black humanity. The Black man is not bad. He is a human being like any other human being whatever the color. It is the world historical situation and the environment which has made him what he is. When Africa is free and united under one Government for the whole of the continent the Black man - wherever he may be - either in Africa, the West Indies or the U.S.A., will discover his personality, his dignity and his honor. Only then will he behave as a complete person, a real human being. So instead of being disgusted, let us work hard together to save his humanity. Let us work hard to give him a strong government of Africa and protect him.

I am well and happy and I am working hard on my next book which I think I will call *Challenge of the Congo*. It may come out in either July or August.

                                  Yours very Sincerely
                                  Kwame Nkrumah

1967   *Challenge of the Congo* published.

1968   *Dark Days in Ghana*, and *The Handbook of Revolutionary Warfare* published, as well as 3 pamphlets.

A LETTER SHARED

No great revolutionary struggles have been won without high cost in suffering and sacrifice, and the violent struggles at present taking place throughout the world are an inevitable phase in the progress towards total liberation. The Black Power movement in the U.S.A. and the African Revolution are one and the same, and nothing can prevent their ultimate fultilment.

```
                                    P.O. Box 834,
                                       Conakry,
                                 Republic of Guinea.

                                 28th July, 1970.
```

Mrs. Christine Johnson,
4349 King Drive,
Chicago,
Illinois 60653,
U.S.A.

Dear Christy,

   I have just received your letter of 10th June, and the award from the Malcolm X Black Hand Society. I am writing to Luqman to thank him and the Society for bestowing this honour on me.

   No great revolutionary struggles have been won without high cost in suffering and sacrifice, and the violent struggles at present taking place throughout the world are an inevitable phase in the progress towards total liberation. The Black Power movement in the U.S.A. and the African Revolution are one and the same, and nothing can prevent their ultimate fulfilment.

   I am in good health, and I hope you are well.

   With best wishes,

                                    Sincerely,